GCSE English

The Merchant of Venice

by William Shakespeare

The Merchant of Venice is a brilliant play, but it's not always easy to understand what's going on. Unless you have this CGP book, of course…

It contains the full text of all five acts — and we've explained all the difficult parts in straightforward, day-to-day English. On top of that, we've added helpful notes about the characters, themes, historical background and more.

We've also included plenty of practice questions to test you on what you've learnt. It's enough to impress even the most learnèd judge.

The Complete Play

CONTENTS

Act One

Act Two

CONTENTS

Published by CGP

Editors:
Alex Fairer
Louise McEvoy
Jack Tooth

With thanks to Paula Barnett and Izzy Bowen for the proofreading.
With thanks to Ana Pungartnik for the copyright research.

Acknowledgements:

With thanks to Photostage for permission to use the images on pages 1, 4, 5, 6, 18, 20, 32, 39, 56 & 68.

With thanks to Alamy for permission to use the images on pages 1, 3, 5, 6 & 14.

With thanks to iStock.com for permission to use the image on page 2.

With thanks to Getty Images for permission to use the image on page 2.

With thanks to Rex Features for permission to use the images on pages 4 & 6.

With thanks to Gulfshore Playhouse for permission to use the images on pages 5, 6, 7, 26, 27 & 30.

Image on page 5: The Cast of Gulfshore Playhouse's 'The Merchant of Venice'. Photographer: Pedro Zepeda.

Image on page 6: Ally Carey and William Oliver Watkins in Gulfshore Playhouse's 'The Merchant of Venice'. Photographer: Pedro Zepeda.

Image on page 6: William Oliver Watkins in Gulfshore Playhouse's 'The Merchant of Venice'. Photographer: Pedro Zepeda.

Image on page 7: William Oliver Watkins and Samuel Ashdown in Gulfshore Playhouse's 'The Merchant of Venice'. Photographer: Pedro Zepeda.

Image on page 26: Jeffrey Binder and Angela Janas in Gulfshore Playhouse's 'The Merchant of Venice'. Photographer: Pedro Zepeda.

Image on page 27: Zachary Martens in Gulfshore Playhouse's 'The Merchant of Venice'. Photographer: Pedro Zepeda.

Image on page 30: Zachary Martens and Angela Janas in Gulfshore Playhouse's 'The Merchant of Venice'. Photographer: Pedro Zepeda.

With thanks to ArenaPAL for permission to use the images on pages 6 & 42.

With thanks to Stewart McPherson for permission to use the images on pages 6 & 34.

With thanks to Shakespeare's Globe for permission to use the image on page 49.

Image on page 49: Jonathan Pryce as Shylock and Dominic Mafham as Antonio in The Merchant of Venice, directed by Jonathan Munby, at Shakespeare's Globe (2015). Photographer credit Manuel Harlan.

ISBN: 978 1 78294 850 6
Printed by Elanders Ltd, Newcastle upon Tyne.
Images and Clipart throughout the book from Corel® and Clipart.com.

Based on the classic CGP style created by Richard Parsons.

Introduction to 'The Merchant of Venice'

The Merchant of Venice is a play by William Shakespeare

- William Shakespeare was an <u>English playwright</u>.

- He wrote some of the <u>most famous</u> plays in the English language, including comedies (such as *<u>Twelfth Night</u>*), tragedies (such as *<u>Romeo and Juliet</u>* and *<u>Hamlet</u>*) and histories (such as *<u>Richard III</u>*).

- *The Merchant of Venice* is one of Shakespeare's <u>comedies</u>. It was written in the <u>1590s</u> and first published in <u>1600</u>.

- The play is about the <u>feud</u> between <u>Antonio</u> and <u>Shylock</u>:

© Donald Cooper/photostage

- Antonio is a <u>wealthy merchant</u> who borrows a large sum of money from Shylock, a <u>vengeful</u> Jewish <u>moneylender</u>.

- Antonio <u>agrees</u> to give Shylock a <u>pound</u> of his own <u>flesh</u> if he doesn't <u>repay</u> the loan <u>in time</u>.

- Antonio <u>gives</u> the money to his friend <u>Bassanio</u>. Bassanio uses it to woo <u>Portia</u>, the woman he <u>loves</u>.

- Antonio <u>can't repay</u> the loan, so Shylock takes him to <u>court</u>.

- Portia <u>intervenes</u> in Antonio's <u>trial</u> and <u>saves</u> his <u>life</u>. Shylock is <u>punished</u> for trying to <u>kill</u> Antonio.

It's a play with a mix of elements

Some of the <u>plot lines</u> in *The Merchant of Venice* are Shakespeare's <u>own invention</u>, but he was also <u>inspired</u> by a <u>wide range</u> of <u>other sources</u>. This helps to make the play <u>varied</u> — it includes lots of <u>different elements</u>:

The most excellent

Historie of the Merchant
of Venice.

VVith the extreame crueltie of Shylocke the Iewe
towards the sayd Merchant, in cutting a iust pound
of his flesh· and the obtayning of Portia
by the choyse of three
chests.

As it hath beene diuers times acted by the Lord
Chamberlaine his Seruants.

Written by William Shakespeare.

AT LONDON,
Printed by *J. R.* for Thomas Heyes,
and are to be sold in Paules Church-yard, at the
signe of the Greene Dragon.
1600

© INTERFOTO / Alamy Stock Photo

- **Humour** —
  The play contains lots of features of a <u>comedy</u>, like <u>mistaken identity</u> and <u>wordplay</u>. Lancelet and his father are only <u>included</u> in the play to make the audience <u>laugh</u>.

- **Tragedy** —
  Although the play is a <u>comedy</u>, many scenes are <u>dark</u> and <u>serious</u>. The <u>prejudice</u> shown to Shylock by the <u>Christian characters</u> is also likely to <u>shock</u> a <u>modern audience</u>.

- **Love** —
  The play features three <u>romantic relationships</u> and several <u>close friendships</u>. These relationships face <u>problems</u> and some of them come into <u>conflict</u> with each other, but <u>ultimately</u> they end <u>well</u>.

- **Hatred** —
  <u>Hatred</u> drives the <u>main plot</u>. Shylock only offers to lend money to Antonio because he senses an <u>opportunity</u> to take <u>revenge</u> on him.

Shakespeare's Theatre

Theatre was popular in Shakespeare's time

- Shakespeare was the <u>most successful</u> playwright of his era, but there was plenty of <u>demand</u> for new plays from other playwrights such as <u>Christopher Marlowe</u> and <u>Thomas Kyd</u>.

- The first successful theatres in London were built in the <u>1570s</u>. Plays attracted <u>large crowds</u>, including the most <u>wealthy</u> in society.

- The theatre wasn't just for rich people — Shakespeare's audiences included <u>servants</u> and <u>labourers</u>. The poorer people in the audience stood in <u>front</u> of the stage — if it rained, they got wet.

- There was <u>no electricity</u>, so most plays were put on <u>during the day</u>.

- There wasn't much <u>scenery</u> and <u>sets</u> were <u>basic</u> so they could be <u>adapted easily</u> to show several different plays.

William Shakespeare

©iStock.com/claudiodivizia

Shakespeare staged his plays at the Globe Theatre

Shakespeare's theatre company performed at the <u>Globe Theatre</u> in London. This is what it might have <u>looked like</u>:

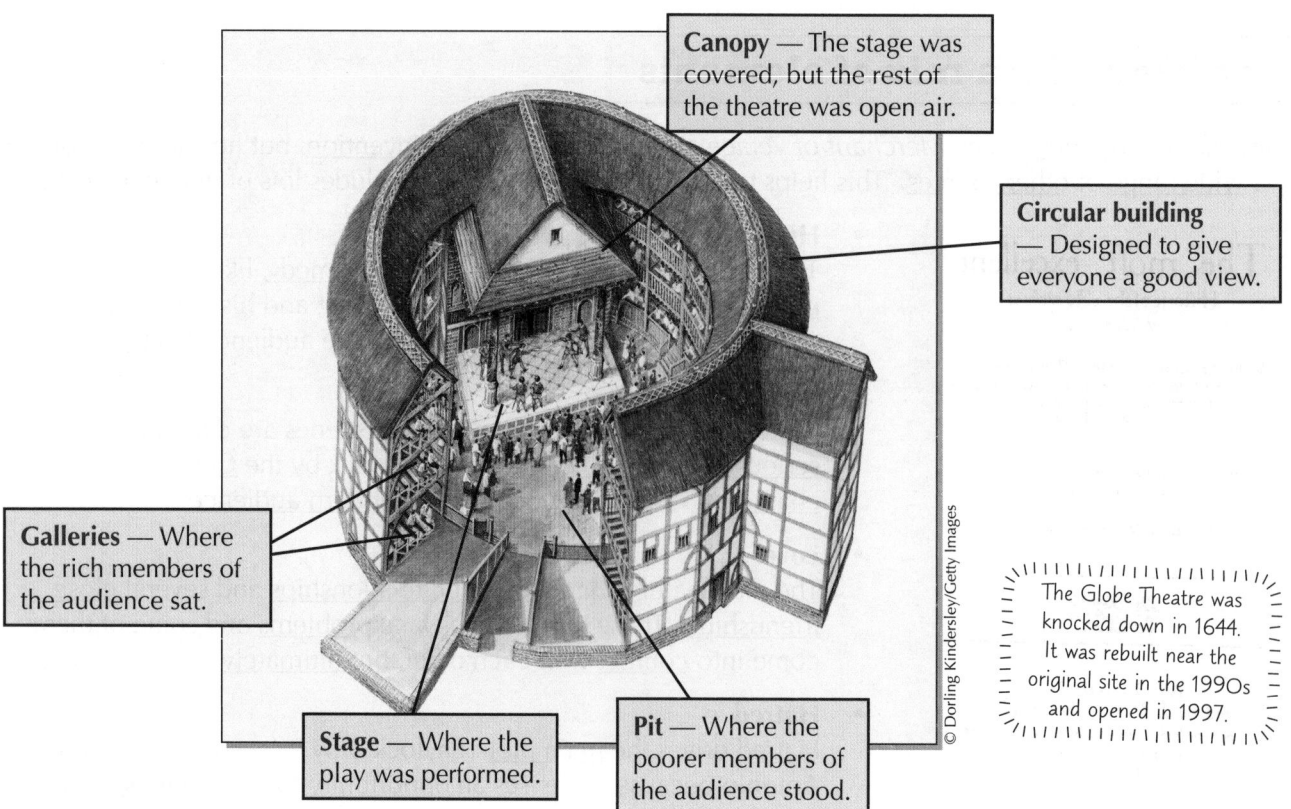

Canopy — The stage was covered, but the rest of the theatre was open air.

Circular building — Designed to give everyone a good view.

Galleries — Where the rich members of the audience sat.

Stage — Where the play was performed.

Pit — Where the poorer members of the audience stood.

© Dorling Kindersley/Getty Images

The Globe Theatre was knocked down in 1644. It was rebuilt near the original site in the 1990s and opened in 1997.

Stagecraft

There's more to the play than just the words

'Stagecraft' is the skill of writing a play so that it works well on stage.

The Merchant of Venice is meant to be <u>watched</u>, not <u>read</u> — when you read the play, <u>imagine</u> how the action would <u>look</u> on stage. You could think about:

Props

- In Act 4, Scene 1, Shylock <u>sharpens a knife</u> using the sole of his shoe. This makes him seem <u>bloodthirsty</u> to the <u>audience</u>.

Stage directions

- The stage directions say that Act 2, Scene 1 starts with a "*<u>Flourish of cornets</u>*". This gives the Prince of Morocco's entrance a <u>ceremonial atmosphere</u>.

In this production, Shylock wears a yellow badge to distinguish him from the Christian characters.

© Vibrant Pictures / Alamy Stock Photo

Costumes

- Many of the characters in the play are <u>wealthy</u>, so in the 1600s they would have worn <u>costumes</u> to match their <u>high status</u>. Shylock might have worn <u>different clothing</u> to show that he's <u>Jewish</u>.

- Disguises feature <u>heavily</u> in the plot, which means <u>some characters</u> have to <u>change costumes</u>. The <u>audience</u> can tell <u>who</u> is wearing these disguises, but the <u>other characters</u> often <u>can't</u>.

Settings

- *The Merchant of Venice* is set in <u>Venice</u>, which was seen as an <u>exotic</u> place in <u>Elizabethan England</u>. It was an important <u>trading</u> city which drew <u>visitors</u> from as far away as the <u>Middle East</u> and <u>China</u>.

- The action also takes place in <u>Belmont</u> — a <u>fictional setting</u> near Venice. Belmont is a <u>peaceful</u> and <u>domestic</u> setting that provides a <u>contrast</u> to the <u>fast-paced</u> and <u>bustling</u> atmosphere of <u>Venice</u>.

Stage directions tell the actors what to do

When you're reading the play, look at the <u>stage directions</u> — they're little phrases in *italics* that tell the actors <u>what</u> to do, <u>when</u> to come in and when to <u>leave</u> the stage.

These are the really <u>common</u> stage directions in <u>Shakespeare</u>:

Enter	=	when someone <u>comes onto</u> the stage
Exit	=	when one person <u>leaves</u> the stage
Exeunt	=	when <u>more</u> than one person <u>leaves</u>
Aside	=	when a character <u>talks</u> to <u>themselves</u>, the <u>audience</u> or a <u>particular</u> character, but <u>not all</u> characters on stage can <u>hear</u>

An 'aside' is a great way for characters to reveal their thoughts to the audience.

Performances of 'The Merchant of Venice'

The Merchant of Venice was created for an Elizabethan stage

A 2015 production of the play in the rebuilt Globe Theatre.

- In Shakespeare's time <u>only men</u> were allowed to <u>act</u> on stage — all the <u>female roles</u> were played by <u>boys</u>.

- Most of the actors would have worn <u>elaborate costumes</u> based on the <u>fashions of the time</u>.

- <u>Musicians</u> helped to create <u>atmosphere</u> in the play. In Act 5, Scene 1, "sweet" music contributes to the <u>romantic</u> atmosphere of <u>Belmont</u> at <u>night</u>.

- Elizabethan <u>theatres</u> could only use <u>basic scenery</u>. Because of this, Shakespeare uses <u>descriptive language</u> to <u>tell</u> the audience <u>when</u> and <u>where</u> the action is <u>happening</u>.

It has been performed for centuries...

The <u>way</u> *The Merchant of Venice* has been performed on stage has <u>changed</u> since <u>Shakespeare's time</u>:

- <u>Women</u> were allowed to <u>perform on stage</u> from <u>1660</u>. Since then, Portia and the other female characters have been played by <u>women</u>.

- <u>Shylock</u> was <u>originally</u> portrayed as a <u>comic villain</u>, but he has generally been played as a more <u>sympathetic</u> character since the <u>early 19th century</u>.

- More recently, *The Merchant of Venice* has been performed in a <u>variety</u> of <u>different ways</u>. In 1994, <u>Peter Sellars</u> directed a performance of the play for the <u>Barbican Theatre</u> in London where the action was set in <u>Venice Beach</u>, <u>California</u>.

... and adapted for stage and screen

The Merchant of Venice has been <u>adapted</u> lots of times:

- <u>Reynaldo Hahn</u> based an <u>opera</u> on the play, which was first performed in 1935. The story was <u>the same</u>, but he <u>left out</u> some of the <u>minor characters</u>, like Lancelet and his father.

- <u>Arnold Wesker</u> reimagined the <u>plot</u> of *The Merchant of Venice* in his own play, *The Merchant* (1976). In Wesker's version, Shylock and Antonio are <u>close friends</u> in spite of their <u>religious differences</u>.

- In 2004, <u>Michael Radford</u> directed a <u>film adaptation</u> starring Jeremy Irons and Al Pacino. He reproduced the <u>atmosphere</u> of the <u>original play</u> by shooting the film <u>on location</u> in Venice.

The 2004 film version of 'The Merchant of Venice'.

Themes and Techniques

The themes are the main ideas of the play

When you write about the play, you'll often have to comment on its themes. Here are the main ones:

Photographer: Pedro Zepeda

- Justice and Mercy — Shylock uses the bond to get justice for the cruel way Antonio has treated him. The Christians urge him to show mercy.
- Love — Love creates happiness and conflict. All of the couples end up happily married, but Bassanio is taught to value his wife over Antonio.
- Wealth — Many of the characters are motivated by money. Portia's large inheritance is part of the reason Bassanio wants to marry her.
- Prejudice — Shylock is abused by the Christian characters for his Jewish faith, and his own hatred for Antonio drives the main plot.
- Reality and Appearance — The play shows that looks can be deceiving. This message is made clear by the casket test set up by Portia's father.

The play's language is important...

© Donald Cooper/photostage

Look out for these techniques as you read the play:

- Poetry and Prose — Shakespeare uses different rhythms of speech for different characters. Most of the characters speak in blank verse, but some of them use prose too.
- Imagery — metaphors, similes and personification make the language rich and interesting. Portia uses lots of religious imagery in her "quality of mercy" speech (Act 4, Scene 1).
- Puns — when words with more than one meaning or two words that sound alike are used to create humour or reveal a character's thoughts. Lancelet uses puns to wind up Lorenzo in Act 3, Scene 5.

... but Shakespeare uses other techniques too

Shakespeare's techniques aren't all language-based — he also uses other dramatic devices:

- Dramatic Irony — when the audience knows something the characters don't. In Act 1, Scene 3, Shylock tells Antonio their bond is "a merry sport", but the audience knows he wants to use it to get revenge.
- Foreshadowing — when Shakespeare hints at what will happen in the play. In Act 1, Scene 1, Salerio describes the dangers faced by ships at sea. This foreshadows the destruction of Antonio's own ships.

And if you wrong us, shall we not revenge?...

Now that you know about the background to *The Merchant of Venice*, it's time to tackle the play itself. Think about the characters, themes and Shakespeare's techniques as you read through the play — and think about stagecraft too...

© United Archives GmbH / Alamy Stock Photo

Introduction

Characters

Many of the characters are good friends

Antonio is a successful merchant.

Shylock is a Jewish moneylender.

Portia is a rich heiress who lives in Belmont.

Bassanio is a close friend of Antonio.

Jessica is Shylock's daughter.

Lorenzo is Jessica's lover.

Nerissa is Portia's lady-in-waiting.

Gratiano is a good friend of Bassanio.

Salerio and **Solanio** are friends to Antonio, Bassanio and the other Christian characters.

Lancelet

The Prince of Morocco

The Prince of Aragon

The Duke of Venice

Act 1, Scene 1 — Bassanio Asks a Favour

Antonio is <u>miserable</u>, but he says he doesn't know <u>why</u>. He discusses the <u>cause</u> of his <u>sadness</u> with Salerio and Solanio. Later in the scene, Bassanio <u>asks</u> Antonio for <u>money</u> — he wants to <u>woo</u> Portia, but he isn't as <u>rich</u> as her <u>other suitors</u>. Antonio <u>agrees</u> to <u>help</u> Bassanio.

Photographer: Pedro Zepeda

ACT 1, SCENE 1

VENICE. A STREET.

Enter ANTONIO, SALERIO *and* SOLANIO

ANTONIO	In sooth, I know not why I am so sad:	
	It wearies me; you say it wearies you;	
	But how I caught it, found it, or came by it,	
	What stuff 'tis made of, whereof it is born,	
	I am to learn;	5
	And such a want-wit sadness makes of me,	
	That I have much ado to know myself.	
SALERIO	Your mind is tossing on the ocean;	
	There, where your argosies with portly sail,	
	Like signiors and rich burghers on the flood,	10
	Or, as it were, the pageants of the sea,	
	Do overpeer the petty traffickers,	
	That curtsy to them, do them reverence,	
	As they fly by them with their woven wings.	
SOLANIO	Believe me, sir, had I such venture forth,	15
	The better part of my affections would	
	Be with my hopes abroad. I should be still	
	Plucking the grass, to know where sits the wind,	
	Peering in maps for ports and piers and roads;	
	And every object that might make me fear	20
	Misfortune to my ventures, out of doubt	
	Would make me sad.	
SALERIO	My wind cooling my broth	
	Would blow me to an ague, when I thought	
	What harm a wind too great might do at sea.	
	I should not see the sandy hour-glass run,	25
	But I should think of shallows and of flats,	
	And see my wealthy *Andrew* docked in sand,	
	Vailing her high-top lower than her ribs	
	To kiss her burial. Should I go to church	
	And see the holy edifice of stone,	30
	And not bethink me straight of dangerous rocks,	
	Which touching but my gentle vessel's side,	
	Would scatter all her spices on the stream,	
	Enrobe the roaring waters with my silks,	
	And, in a word, but even now worth this,	35
	And now worth nothing? Shall I have the thought	
	To think on this, and shall I lack the thought	
	That such a thing bechanced would make me sad?	
	But tell not me; I know, Antonio	
	Is sad to think upon his merchandise.	40

1 'In sooth' means 'in truth'.

Shakespeare's Techniques

Antonio's <u>sadness</u> creates an <u>uneasy atmosphere</u> at the start of the play. This is <u>unusual</u> for a <u>comedy</u>.

6-7 'And this ridiculous sadness makes me doubt how well I know myself.'

9-12 'where your majestic ships, like wealthy and distinguished gentlemen, look down on the smaller boats around them'.

13 'do them reverence' means 'show them respect'.

15-17 'I'd be worried too if I had as many ships at sea as you.'

22-24 'I'd shiver every time I blew on my soup to cool it down, as it would make me think of the damage a strong wind could do to my ships.'

27-29 'grounded in the sand — the mast lowering itself to the ground to meet its resting place.'

30 'edifice' means 'building'.

Theme — Wealth

Salerio and Solanio <u>assume</u> that Antonio is worried by his <u>business</u>. This shows that <u>money</u> is often at the <u>forefront</u> of their thinking.

42-44 'My business doesn't rely on a single ship or on one part of the world — I won't run out of money if this year doesn't go well'.

47 'Fie, fie!' is an exclamation of mild disgust or disapproval.

51 Janus was a Roman god who had two faces.

55 'vinegar aspect' means 'a sour-faced expression'.

57 In Greek mythology, Nestor was a king known for his wisdom.

Theme — Love

The audience is introduced to several male friendships in this scene. These men are openly affectionate and value each other's company.

68 'We never see each other these days — does it have to be that way?'

75-76 'You worry too much — it stops you from enjoying life'.

Character — Antonio

Antonio's sadness makes him stand out from the other characters. This also happens in the final scene.

83 'mortifying' means 'deadly'.

ANTONIO	Believe me, no: I thank my fortune for it, My ventures are not in one bottom trusted, Nor to one place; nor is my whole estate Upon the fortune of this present year: Therefore my merchandise makes me not sad. 45
SALERIO	Why, then you are in love.
ANTONIO	Fie, fie!
SALERIO	Not in love neither? Then let us say you are sad, Because you are not merry: and 'twere as easy For you to laugh and leap and say you are merry, 50 Because you are not sad. Now, by two-headed Janus, Nature hath framed strange fellows in her time: Some that will evermore peep through their eyes And laugh like parrots at a bag-piper, And other of such vinegar aspect 55 That they'll not show their teeth in way of smile, Though Nestor swear the jest be laughable.

Enter BASSANIO, LORENZO *and* GRATIANO

SOLANIO	Here comes Bassanio, your most noble kinsman, Gratiano and Lorenzo. Fare ye well: We leave you now with better company. 60
SALERIO	I would have stayed till I had made you merry, If worthier friends had not prevented me.
ANTONIO	Your worth is very dear in my regard. I take it, your own business calls on you And you embrace the occasion to depart. 65
SALERIO	Good morrow, my good lords.
BASSANIO	Good signiors both, when shall we laugh? Say, when? You grow exceeding strange: must it be so?
SALERIO	We'll make our leisures to attend on yours.

Exeunt SALERIO *and* SOLANIO

LORENZO	My Lord Bassanio, since you have found Antonio, 70 We two will leave you: but at dinnertime, I pray you, have in mind where we must meet.
BASSANIO	I will not fail you.
GRATIANO	You look not well, Signior Antonio; You have too much respect upon the world: 75 They lose it that do buy it with much care: Believe me, you are marvellously changed.
ANTONIO	I hold the world but as the world, Gratiano; A stage where every man must play a part, And mine a sad one.
GRATIANO	Let me play the fool: 80 With mirth and laughter let old wrinkles come, And let my liver rather heat with wine Than my heart cool with mortifying groans.

Act 1, Scene 1

	Why should a man, whose blood is warm within,	
	Sit like his grandsire cut in alabaster?	85
	Sleep when he wakes and creep into the jaundice	
	By being peevish? I tell thee what, Antonio —	
	I love thee, and it is my love that speaks —	
	There are a sort of men whose visages	
	Do cream and mantle like a standing pond,	90
	And do a wilful stillness entertain,	
	With purpose to be dressed in an opinion	
	Of wisdom, gravity, profound conceit,	
	As who should say 'I am, sir, an oracle,	
	And when I ope my lips let no dog bark!'	95
	O my Antonio, I do know of these	
	That therefore only are reputed wise	
	For saying nothing; when, I am very sure,	
	If they should speak, would almost damn those ears,	
	Which, hearing them, would call their brothers fools.	100
	I'll tell thee more of this another time:	
	But fish not, with this melancholy bait,	
	For this fool gudgeon, this opinion.	
	Come, good Lorenzo. Fare ye well awhile:	
	I'll end my exhortation after dinner.	105
LORENZO	Well, we will leave you then till dinnertime.	
	(To Antonio and Bassanio) I must be one of these same dumb wise men,	
	For Gratiano never lets me speak.	
GRATIANO	Well, keep me company but two years more,	
	Thou shalt not know the sound of thine own tongue.	110
ANTONIO	Farewell: I'll grow a talker for this gear.	
GRATIANO	Thanks, i' faith, for silence is only commendable	
	In a neat's tongue dried and a maid not vendible.	

Exeunt GRATIANO *and* LORENZO

ANTONIO	Is that anything now?	
BASSANIO	Gratiano speaks an infinite deal of nothing, more than any man in all Venice. His reasons are as two grains of wheat hid in two bushels of chaff: you shall seek all day ere you find them, and when you have them, they are not worth the search.	115 / 120
ANTONIO	Well, tell me now what lady is the same To whom you swore a secret pilgrimage, That you today promised to tell me of?	
BASSANIO	'Tis not unknown to you, Antonio, How much I have disabled mine estate, By something showing a more swelling port Than my faint means would grant continuance: Nor do I now make moan to be abridged From such a noble rate; but my chief care Is to come fairly off from the great debts	125 / 130

Character — Gratiano

Gratiano is presented as a light-hearted character. Here, he mocks the way that some men act serious to convince others that they're wise.

Shakespeare's Techniques

The mood of the scene changes after Gratiano and Lorenzo have left — their jokes make way for a more serious conversation.

84-85 'Why should a man who's alive and well sit like a statue of his grandfather?'

87 'peevish' means 'grumpy'.

89 'visages' means 'faces'.

102-103 'Don't seek the approval of those fools by acting miserable.'

105 'exhortation' means 'lecture'.

111 'I'll talk more from now on.'

112-113 'only dried cows' tongues and undesirable women should stay silent.'

114 'What was he talking about?'

124-127 'You know that I've run out of money by spending more of it than I could afford'.

129-132 'my main concern is to pay off the debts that my lavish lifestyle has got me into.'

Act One

Act 1, Scene 1

Wherein my time something too prodigal
Hath left me gaged. To you, Antonio,
I owe the most, in money and in love,
And from your love I have a warranty
To unburden all my plots and purposes   135
How to get clear of all the debts I owe.

ANTONIO   I pray you, good Bassanio, let me know it;
And if it stand, as you yourself still do,
Within the eye of honour, be assured,
My purse, my person, my extremest means,   140
Lie all unlocked to your occasions.

BASSANIO   In my schooldays, when I had lost one shaft,
I shot his fellow of the self-same flight
The self-same way with more advisèd watch,
To find the other forth, and by adventuring both   145
I oft found both: I urge this childhood proof,
Because what follows is pure innocence.
I owe you much, and, like a wilful youth,
That which I owe is lost; but if you please
To shoot another arrow that self way   150
Which you did shoot the first, I do not doubt,
As I will watch the aim, or to find both
Or bring your latter hazard back again
And thankfully rest debtor for the first.

ANTONIO   You know me well, and herein spend but time   155
To wind about my love with circumstance;
And out of doubt you do me now more wrong
In making question of my uttermost
Than if you had made waste of all I have:
Then do but say to me what I should do   160
That in your knowledge may by me be done,
And I am pressed unto it: therefore, speak.

BASSANIO   In Belmont is a lady richly left;
And she is fair, and, fairer than that word,
Of wondrous virtues: sometimes from her eyes   165
I did receive fair speechless messages:
Her name is Portia, nothing undervalued
To Cato's daughter, Brutus' Portia:
Nor is the wide world ignorant of her worth,
For the four winds blow in from every coast   170
Renownèd suitors, and her sunny locks
Hang on her temples like a golden fleece;
Which makes her seat of Belmont Colchos' strand,
And many Jasons come in quest of her.
O my Antonio, had I but the means   175
To hold a rival place with one of them,
I have a mind presages me such thrift,
That I should questionless be fortunate!

ANTONIO   Thou know'st that all my fortunes are at sea;
Neither have I money nor commodity   180
To raise a present sum: therefore go forth;

Act 1, Scene 2 — Portia is Frustrated

Try what my credit can in Venice do:
That shall be racked, even to the uttermost,
To furnish thee to Belmont, to fair Portia.
Go, presently inquire, and so will I,   185
Where money is, and I no question make
To have it of my trust or for my sake.

Exeunt

182 In other words — 'See if anyone in Venice is willing to lend me the money you need'.

185-187 'Go and see if you can find someone to lend the money, and I'll do the same. It can be a business loan or as a personal favour — I don't mind which.'

Portia is unhappy about having no say in who she marries. Before he died, her father set up a test involving a gold casket, a silver casket and a lead casket — whoever picks the correct casket gets to marry Portia. Several suitors have already come to Belmont, but Portia didn't like any of them. Fortunately for her, they all refused to take the test.

ACT 1, SCENE 2

Character — Nerissa

Nerissa is the person Portia turns to when she's unhappy. She acts as a source of advice here and elsewhere in the play.

BELMONT. A ROOM IN PORTIA'S HOUSE.

Enter PORTIA *and* NERISSA

PORTIA   By my troth, Nerissa, my little body is aweary of this great world.

NERISSA   You would be, sweet madam, if your miseries were in the same abundance as your good fortunes are: and yet, for aught I see, they are as   5
sick that surfeit with too much as they that starve with nothing. It is no mean happiness therefore, to be seated in the mean: superfluity comes sooner by white hairs, but competency lives longer.   10

PORTIA   Good sentences and well pronounced.

NERISSA   They would be better, if well followed.

PORTIA   If to do were as easy as to know what were good to do, chapels had been churches and poor men's cottages princes' palaces. It is a good divine that   15
follows his own instructions: I can easier teach twenty what were good to be done, than be one of the twenty to follow mine own teaching. The brain may devise laws for the blood, but a hot temper leaps o'er a cold decree: such a hare is   20
madness the youth, to skip o'er the meshes of good counsel the cripple. But this reasoning is not in the fashion to choose me a husband. O me, the word 'choose'! I may neither choose whom I would nor refuse whom I dislike; so is the   25
will of a living daughter curbed by the will of a dead father. Is it not hard, Nerissa, that I cannot choose one nor refuse none?

1 'By my troth' means 'I swear'.

1 'aweary' means 'tired'.

6 'surfeit with too much' means 'eat too much'.

7-10 'The key to happiness is being somewhere in the middle — those with too much age more quickly than those with just enough to live.'

13-15 'If doing the right thing was as easy as knowing the right thing to do, we'd all be much better off.'

19-22 'passion can't be reined in by sensible advice. Young people are hares and good advice is an old person failing to trap them'.

Context — Marriage

In the 16th century, it was common for women to have no say in who they married — their families often made the decision.

Act One

Act 1, Scene 2

NERISSA	Your father was ever virtuous; and holy men at their death have good inspirations: therefore the lottery, that he hath devised in these three chests of gold, silver and lead, whereof who chooses his meaning chooses you, will, no doubt, never be chosen by any rightly but one who shall rightly love. But what warmth is there in your affection towards any of these princely suitors that are already come?	30
		35
PORTIA	I pray thee, overname them; and as thou namest them, I will describe them; and, according to my description, level at my affection.	40
NERISSA	First, there is the Neapolitan prince.	
PORTIA	Ay, that's a colt indeed, for he doth nothing but talk of his horse; and he makes it a great appropriation to his own good parts, that he can shoe him himself. I am much afeard my lady his mother played false with a smith.	45
NERISSA	Then there is the County Palatine.	
PORTIA	He doth nothing but frown, as who should say 'If you will not have me, choose'. He hears merry tales and smiles not: I fear he will prove the weeping philosopher when he grows old, being so full of unmannerly sadness in his youth. I had rather be married to a death's-head with a bone in his mouth than to either of these. God defend me from these two!	50
		55
NERISSA	How say you by the French lord, Monsieur Le Bon?	
PORTIA	God made him, and therefore let him pass for a man. In truth, I know it is a sin to be a mocker: but, he! Why, he hath a horse better than the Neapolitan's, a better bad habit of frowning than the Count Palatine; he is every man in no man; if a throstle sing, he falls straight a capering: he will fence with his own shadow: if I should marry him, I should marry twenty husbands. If he would despise me I would forgive him, for if he love me to madness, I shall never requite him.	60
		65
NERISSA	What say you, then, to Falconbridge, the young baron of England?	
PORTIA	You know I say nothing to him, for he understands not me, nor I him: he hath neither Latin, French, nor Italian, and you will come into the court and swear that I have a poor pennyworth in the English. He is a proper man's picture, but, alas, who can converse with a dumb-show? How oddly he is suited! I think he bought his doublet in Italy, his round hose in France, his bonnet in Germany and his behaviour everywhere.	70
		75
NERISSA	What think you of the Scottish lord, his neighbour?	

30 'inspirations' means 'ideas'.

35-37 'What do you think of the suitors who have already visited?'

39-40 'you can guess how much I like them from my descriptions.'

41 'Neapolitan' means 'of Naples' (a city in Italy).

46 'cheated on his father with a blacksmith'.

47 'County Palatine' was a title given to noblemen in many European countries.

52 'unmannerly' means 'impolite'.

53 'death's-head' means 'skull'.

Character — Portia

Portia's descriptions of her suitors are critical, but also light-hearted. Her insults show she's a witty character.

62 A 'throstle' is a 'thrush' (a small songbird).

62 'capering' means 'dancing'.

64-66 'I wouldn't mind if he hated me, because I couldn't love him back if he loved me.'

Shakespeare's Techniques

Portia claims to be bad at speaking English, but that's the language the play is performed in. This creates humour for the audience.

73 'alas' means 'unfortunately'.

Act One

Act 1, Scene 2

PORTIA	That he hath a neighbourly charity in him, for he borrowed a box of the ear of the Englishman and swore he would pay him again when he was able: I think the Frenchman became his surety and sealed under for another.	80
NERISSA	How like you the young German, the Duke of Saxony's nephew?	85
PORTIA	Very vilely in the morning, when he is sober, and most vilely in the afternoon, when he is drunk: when he is best, he is a little worse than a man, and when he is worst, he is little better than a beast: and the worst fall that ever fell, I hope I shall make shift to go without him.	90
NERISSA	If he should offer to choose, and choose the right casket, you should refuse to perform your father's will, if you should refuse to accept him.	
PORTIA	Therefore, for fear of the worst, I pray thee, set a deep glass of Rhenish wine on the contrary casket, for if the devil be within and that temptation without, I know he will choose it. I will do anything, Nerissa, ere I'll be married to a sponge.	95 / 100
NERISSA	You need not fear, lady, the having any of these lords: they have acquainted me with their determinations; which is, indeed, to return to their home and to trouble you with no more suit, unless you may be won by some other sort than your father's imposition depending on the caskets.	105
PORTIA	If I live to be as old as Sibylla, I will die as chaste as Diana, unless I be obtained by the manner of my father's will. I am glad this parcel of wooers are so reasonable, for there is not one among them but I dote on his very absence, and I pray God grant them a fair departure.	110
NERISSA	Do you not remember, lady, in your father's time, a Venetian, a scholar and a soldier, that came hither in company of the Marquis of Montferrat?	115
PORTIA	Yes, yes, it was Bassanio; as I think, he was so called.	
NERISSA	True, madam: he, of all the men that ever my foolish eyes looked upon, was the best deserving a fair lady.	120
PORTIA	I remember him well, and I remember him worthy of thy praise.	
	Enter a Servant	
	How now! What news?	
SERVANT	The four strangers seek for you, madam, to take their leave: and there is a forerunner come from a fifth, the Prince of Morocco, who brings word the	125

Shakespeare's Techniques

The humour of this scene relies mainly on national stereotypes. This remark refers to an Elizabethan belief that the Scottish often got the French to fight their battles for them.

79-80 'he got hit on the ear by the Englishman'.

82 In other words — 'I think the Frenchman promised to hit the Englishman back on his behalf'.

90-91 'if he died, I think I'd manage to live without him.'

96 Rhenish is a type of wine from the region surrounding the Rhine (a German river).

100 'sponge' means 'drunkard'.

103 'determinations' means 'intentions'.

107 In Greek mythology, Sibylla was a prophetess who lived for a thousand years.

108 Diana was a Roman goddess linked to chastity (sexual purity).

110-111 'there isn't one of them I'm sad to see go'.

Character — Bassanio

Just like Bassanio's praise of Portia (Act 1, Scene 1) gives the audience a good impression of her, Portia's fond memory of Bassanio makes him seem likeable.

126 Morocco is an Arabic country in northern Africa.

Act One

Act 1, Scene 3 — The Loan is Agreed

132 'shrive me' means 'listen to my confession'.

PORTIA	prince his master will be here tonight.
PORTIA	If I could bid the fifth welcome with so good a heart as I can bid the other four farewell, I should be glad of his approach: if he have the condition of a saint and the complexion of a devil, I had rather he should shrive me than wive me. Come, Nerissa. (*To the Servingman*) Sirrah, go before. Whiles we shut the gates upon one wooer, another knocks at the door.

130

135

Exeunt

Bassanio asks Shylock for a <u>loan</u> of three thousand ducats <u>in Antonio's name</u>. Shylock <u>agrees</u> to lend the money, but there's <u>one condition</u> — Antonio has to give up a pound of his <u>flesh</u> if he doesn't <u>repay</u> it <u>in time</u>. Shylock plans to use the loan to take <u>revenge</u> on Antonio for <u>mistreating</u> him <u>in the past</u>.

© Vibrant Pictures / Alamy Stock Photo

1 'ducats' are gold coins.

13 'imputation' means 'accusation'.

17 'argosy' means 'ship'.

17 Tripolis (Tripoli) is a port on the north coast of Africa.

18 The Rialto was a small island that acted as the centre of trade in 16th-century Venice.

20 'squandered' means 'scattered'.

ACT 1, SCENE 3

VENICE. A PUBLIC PLACE.

Enter BASSANIO *and* SHYLOCK

SHYLOCK	Three thousand ducats; well.
BASSANIO	Ay, sir, for three months.
SHYLOCK	For three months; well.
BASSANIO	For the which, as I told you, Antonio shall be bound.
SHYLOCK	Antonio shall become bound; well.
BASSANIO	May you stead me? Will you pleasure me? Shall I know your answer?
SHYLOCK	Three thousand ducats for three months and Antonio bound.
BASSANIO	Your answer to that.
SHYLOCK	Antonio is a good man.
BASSANIO	Have you heard any imputation to the contrary?
SHYLOCK	Oh, no, no, no, no: my meaning in saying he is a good man is to have you understand me that he is sufficient. Yet his means are in supposition: he hath an argosy bound to Tripolis, another to the Indies; I understand moreover, upon the Rialto, he hath a third at Mexico, a fourth for England, and other ventures he hath, squandered abroad. But ships are but boards, sailors but men: there be land-rats and water-rats, water-thieves and

5

10

15

20

Act One

Act 1, Scene 3

	land-thieves, I mean pirates, and then there is the peril of waters, winds and rocks. The man is, notwithstanding, sufficient. Three thousand ducats; I think I may take his bond.	25
BASSANIO	Be assured you may.	
SHYLOCK	I will be assured I may; and, that I may be assured, I will bethink me. May I speak with Antonio?	30
BASSANIO	If it please you to dine with us.	
SHYLOCK	Yes, to smell pork; to eat of the habitation which your prophet the Nazarite conjured the devil into. I will buy with you, sell with you, talk with you, walk with you, and so following, but I will not eat with you, drink with you, nor pray with you. What news on the Rialto? Who is he comes here?	35

Enter ANTONIO

| BASSANIO | This is Signior Antonio. | |
| SHYLOCK | *(Aside)* How like a fawning publican he looks! I hate him for he is a Christian, But more for that in low simplicity He lends out money gratis and brings down The rate of usance here with us in Venice. If I can catch him once upon the hip, I will feed fat the ancient grudge I bear him. He hates our sacred nation, and he rails, Even there where merchants most do congregate, On me, my bargains and my well-won thrift, Which he calls interest. Cursèd be my tribe, If I forgive him! | 40

45 |
| BASSANIO | Shylock, do you hear? | 50 |
| SHYLOCK | I am debating of my present store, And, by the near guess of my memory, I cannot instantly raise up the gross Of full three thousand ducats. What of that? Tubal, a wealthy Hebrew of my tribe, Will furnish me. But soft! How many months Do you desire? *(To Antonio)* Rest you fair, good signior; Your worship was the last man in our mouths. |

55 |
ANTONIO	Shylock, although I neither lend nor borrow By taking nor by giving of excess, Yet, to supply the ripe wants of my friend, I'll break a custom. *(To Bassanio)* Is he yet possessed How much ye would?	60
SHYLOCK	Ay, ay, three thousand ducats.	
ANTONIO	And for three months.	65
SHYLOCK	I had forgot; three months; you told me so. Well then, your bond; and let me see; but hear you;	

Context — Judaism

Jewish food laws forbid Jews to eat pork. Shylock's disgust at Bassanio's offer shows the cultural divide between Jews and Christians in 16th-century Venice.

33 'the Nazarite' refers to Jesus Christ, who grew up in Nazareth. According to the Bible, Jesus drove out demons from a possessed man and sent them into a herd of pigs.

39 'He looks just like a snivelling tax collector!'

Character — Shylock

Shylock hates Antonio partly because he lends money without charging interest. This harms Shylock's business by reducing the interest he can ask for on his loans.

46 'He hates all Jewish people'.

Theme — Justice and Mercy

Shylock believes he would be letting other Jews down if he didn't seek justice for the horrible way Antonio has treated him. He thinks that revenge is the only way to achieve this justice.

53 'gross' means 'sum'.

55 'Hebrew' means 'Jew'.

58 'We were just talking about you.'

62-63 'Does he already know how much money you need?'

Act 1, Scene 3

69 'Upon advantage' means 'with interest'.

Context — Jacob and Laban

Shylock refers to a biblical story to make his point — Jacob used his intelligence to make a profit (his uncle's lambs). Shylock doesn't think charging interest is wrong — to him, it's a way of making profit like Jacob.

77-79 'Once Jacob had agreed with Laban that any newborn lambs with stripes or spots would belong to him'.

81 'generation' means 'mating'.

83-85 'Jacob stripped the bark from some branches and put them in the ground in front of the mating sheep'. (The idea was that these striped and spotted branches would give the newborn lambs stripes and spots).

87 'Fall' means 'give birth to'.

Theme — Prejudice

Antonio argues that Jacob's success was the work of God. His different view emphasises the difference between Antonio and Shylock's religious beliefs.

Shakespeare's Techniques

Antonio regularly interrupts Shylock. This increases the tension between them.

107 'rated' means 'criticised'.

112 A 'gaberdine' is a type of cloak.

Methought you said you neither lend nor borrow
Upon advantage.

ANTONIO   I do never use it.

SHYLOCK When Jacob grazed his uncle Laban's sheep —   70
This Jacob from our holy Abram was,
As his wise mother wrought in his behalf,
The third possessor; ay, he was the third —

ANTONIO And what of him? Did he take interest?

SHYLOCK No, not take interest, not, as you would say,   75
Directly interest: mark what Jacob did.
When Laban and himself were compromised
That all the eanlings which were streaked and pied
Should fall as Jacob's hire, the ewes, being rank,
In the end of autumn turnèd to the rams,   80
And, when the work of generation was
Between these woolly breeders in the act,
The skilful shepherd peeled me certain wands,
And, in the doing of the deed of kind,
He stuck them up before the fulsome ewes,   85
Who then conceiving did in eaning time
Fall parti-coloured lambs, and those were Jacob's.
This was a way to thrive, and he was blest:
And thrift is blessing, if men steal it not.

ANTONIO This was a venture, sir, that Jacob served for;   90
A thing not in his power to bring to pass,
But swayed and fashioned by the hand of heaven.
Was this inserted to make interest good?
Or is your gold and silver ewes and rams?

SHYLOCK I cannot tell; I make it breed as fast: 95
But note me, signior —

ANTONIO   Mark you this, Bassanio,
The devil can cite Scripture for his purpose.
An evil soul producing holy witness
Is like a villain with a smiling cheek,   100
A goodly apple rotten at the heart:
O, what a goodly outside falsehood hath!

SHYLOCK Three thousand ducats; 'tis a good round sum.
Three months from twelve; then, let me see; the
rate —

ANTONIO Well, Shylock, shall we be beholding to you?   105

SHYLOCK Signior Antonio, many a time and oft
In the Rialto you have rated me
About my moneys and my usances:
Still have I borne it with a patient shrug,
For sufferance is the badge of all our tribe.   110
You call me misbeliever, cut-throat dog,
And spit upon my Jewish gaberdine,
And all for use of that which is mine own.
Well then, it now appears you need my help:
Go to, then; you come to me, and you say   115

'Shylock, we would have moneys' — you say so;
You, that did void your rheum upon my beard
And foot me as you spurn a stranger cur
Over your threshold. Moneys is your suit;
What should I say to you? Should I not say   120
'Hath a dog money? Is it possible
A cur can lend three thousand ducats?' Or
Shall I bend low and in a bondman's key,
With bated breath and whispering humbleness,
Say this; 'Fair sir, you spat on me on Wednesday
                                           last; 125
You spurned me such a day; another time
You called me dog; and for these courtesies
I'll lend you thus much moneys'?

ANTONIO   I am as like to call thee so again,
To spit on thee again, to spurn thee too.   130
If thou wilt lend this money, lend it not
As to thy friends; for when did friendship take
A breed for barren metal of his friend?
But lend it rather to thine enemy,
Who, if he break, thou mayst with better face   135
Exact the penalty.

SHYLOCK   Why, look you, how you storm!
I would be friends with you and have your love,
Forget the shames that you have stained me with,
Supply your present wants and take no doit
Of usance for my moneys, and you'll not hear me: 140
This is kind I offer.

BASSANIO   This were kindness.

SHYLOCK   This kindness will I show.
Go with me to a notary, seal me there
Your single bond; and, in a merry sport,
If you repay me not on such a day,   145
In such a place, such sum or sums as are
Expressed in the condition, let the forfeit
Be nominated for an equal pound
Of your fair flesh, to be cut off and taken
In what part of your body pleaseth me.   150

ANTONIO   Content, i' faith: I'll seal to such a bond
And say there is much kindness in the Jew.

BASSANIO   You shall not seal to such a bond for me:
I'll rather dwell in my necessity.

ANTONIO   Why, fear not, man; I will not forfeit it: 155
Within these two months, that's a month before
This bond expires, I do expect return
Of thrice three times the value of this bond.

SHYLOCK   O father Abram, what these Christians are,
Whose own hard dealings teaches them suspect   160
The thoughts of others! Pray you, tell me this;
If he should break his day, what should I gain

117-119 'You, who spat on my beard and kicked me like you'd kick a stray dog from your house.'

123 'in a bondman's key' means 'in a slave's tone'.

Character — Shylock
Shylock is the villain of the play, but the way Antonio treats him might make a modern audience feel sympathy for him.

132-133 'what kind of person charges their friends interest?'

135 'break' means 'fails to repay'.

139-140 'I'm offering you the money you need without even a penny of interest, but you're not listening to me'.

143 A 'notary' was someone who drew up legal contracts.

144 'in a merry sport' means 'as a bit of fun'.

153-154 'I won't let you agree to these terms — I would prefer not to have the money at all'.

Shakespeare's Techniques
Antonio's loan is given a time limit. This builds tension by introducing the possibility that he won't be able to repay it on time.

Act 1, Scene 3

163 The 'forfeiture' is the penalty Antonio faces if he can't repay the loan in time (i.e. a pound of flesh).

164-166 'A pound of human flesh is less valuable to me than the flesh of a sheep, cow or goat.'

171 'forthwith' means 'at once'.

175 'unthrifty knave' means 'careless rascal'. Shylock is talking about Lancelet here.

Shakespeare's Techniques

Antonio <u>jokes</u> that the <u>only</u> possible <u>explanation</u> for Shylock's <u>kindness</u> is that he's turning into a <u>Christian</u>. This <u>foreshadows</u> Shylock's <u>forced conversion</u> in Act 4.

Character — Antonio

Salerio and Solanio described the <u>dangers</u> of Antonio's <u>business</u> in Act 1, Scene 1. Antonio seems <u>overconfident</u> for being so sure of his ships' <u>safe return</u>.

	By the exaction of the forfeiture?	
	A pound of man's flesh taken from a man	
	Is not so estimable, profitable neither,	165
	As flesh of muttons, beefs, or goats. I say,	
	To buy his favour, I extend this friendship:	
	If he will take it, so; if not, adieu;	
	And, for my love, I pray you wrong me not.	
ANTONIO	Yes Shylock, I will seal unto this bond.	170
SHYLOCK	Then meet me forthwith at the notary's;	
	Give him direction for this merry bond,	
	And I will go and purse the ducats straight,	
	See to my house, left in the fearful guard	
	Of an unthrifty knave, and presently	175
	I will be with you.	
ANTONIO	Hie thee, gentle Jew.	

Exit SHYLOCK

	The Hebrew will turn Christian: he grows kind.	
BASSANIO	I like not fair terms and a villain's mind.	
ANTONIO	Come on: in this there can be no dismay;	
	My ships come home a month before the day.	180

Exeunt

Shakespeare's Techniques — Poetry and Prose

Most of *The Merchant of Venice* is written in <u>blank verse</u>. Blank verse is a type of poetry that has <u>three main features</u>:

- The lines don't usually <u>rhyme</u>.

- Each line has around <u>ten syllables</u>.

- Each line has five <u>stressed syllables</u> — "What <u>harm</u> a <u>wind</u> too <u>great</u> might <u>do</u> at <u>sea</u>."

The fact that most of the play is written in <u>blank verse</u> means it <u>stands out</u> when characters use <u>prose</u> instead. Prose doesn't <u>rhyme</u> or follow a <u>set rhythm</u>, which makes it sound like <u>everyday speech</u>. In Act 1, Scene 2, <u>Portia</u> and <u>Nerissa</u> speak <u>entirely</u> in prose — this shows how <u>close</u> and <u>comfortable</u> they are with each other.

© Donald Cooper/photostage

Act One — Practice Questions

Quick Questions

1) What two explanations do Salerio and Solanio give for Antonio's sadness?

2) Who is described as Antonio's "most noble kinsman"?

3) Why does Bassanio need to borrow money off Antonio?

4) Do Portia and Nerissa speak in blank verse or prose in Act 1, Scene 2? How can you tell?

5) Why can't Portia choose who she marries?

6) 'Bassanio has never visited Belmont before.' Is this statement true or false?

7) How much money does Bassanio ask Shylock for?

8) Give two reasons why Shylock hates Antonio.

9) Why isn't Antonio worried about repaying Shylock on time?

In-depth Questions

1) Using Act 1 as a starting point, describe these characters' personalities using one word:
   a) Antonio   b) Bassanio   c) Gratiano   d) Portia   e) Nerissa   f) Shylock

2) How does Shakespeare portray the relationship between the Christian men in Act 1, Scene 1?

3) Compare Antonio and Bassanio's attitudes to money in Act 1, Scene 1.

4) In Act 1, Scene 2, how does Shakespeare present Portia's feelings about the casket test? What effect might this have on the audience's opinion of her?

5) Give one example of how Shakespeare creates humour in Act 1, Scene 2.

6) How does Shakespeare present Portia and Nerissa's relationship in Act 1, Scene 2?

7) Explain how Shakespeare builds tension between Antonio and Shylock in Act 1, Scene 3.

8) Reread Act 1, Scene 3 (lines 106-128). Rewrite these lines in modern English.

9) Write a diary entry for Bassanio explaining how he feels at the end of Act 1, Scene 3. Include his feelings for Portia, as well as his thoughts about Antonio and Shylock.

Act 2, Scene 1 — Morocco Makes an Entrance

© Donald Cooper/photostage

The Prince of Morocco <u>brags</u> about his <u>good looks</u> and <u>military achievements</u>. Portia <u>warns</u> him about the <u>consequences</u> of <u>failing</u> the <u>test of the caskets</u>.

Shakespeare's Techniques

A "*Flourish of cornets*" is a <u>short blast</u> of <u>trumpets</u>. Shakespeare uses it to give this scene (and later scenes) a <u>ceremonial atmosphere</u>.

1-3 'Don't hold my skin colour against me — I only look like this because I live so close to the sun.'

5 Phoebus was the Roman sun god, so 'Phoebus' fire' means 'the sun'.

8-9 'I'm telling you, my face strikes fear into the hearts of brave men'.

13-14 'Good looks aren't the only thing I'm looking for in a husband'.

17 'scanted' means 'limited'.

18 'hedged' means 'confined'.

24-26 'I swear by my sword, which killed the Persian ruler and a Persian prince who had already won three battles against the Sultan Suleiman'.

Character — The Prince of Morocco

The prince <u>exaggerates</u> his <u>bravery</u> to <u>impress</u> Portia, but the <u>hyperbole</u> in his speech makes him seem <u>arrogant</u> to the audience.

32 Hercules is a hero from Greek and Roman mythology. Lichas was one of his servants.

35 Alcides is another name for Hercules.

ACT 2, SCENE 1

BELMONT. A ROOM IN PORTIA'S HOUSE.

Flourish of cornets. Enter the PRINCE OF MOROCCO *and his train, with* PORTIA, NERISSA *and others attending.*

MOROCCO	Mislike me not for my complexion,
	The shadowed livery of the burnished sun,
	To whom I am a neighbour and near bred.
	Bring me the fairest creature northward born,
	Where Phoebus' fire scarce thaws the icicles, 5
	And let us make incision for your love,
	To prove whose blood is reddest, his or mine.
	I tell thee, lady, this aspect of mine
	Hath feared the valiant: by my love I swear
	The best-regarded virgins of our clime 10
	Have loved it too: I would not change this hue,
	Except to steal your thoughts, my gentle queen.
PORTIA	In terms of choice I am not solely led
	By nice direction of a maiden's eyes;
	Besides, the lottery of my destiny 15
	Bars me the right of voluntary choosing:
	But if my father had not scanted me
	And hedged me by his wit, to yield myself
	His wife who wins me by that means I told you,
	Yourself, renownèd prince, then stood as fair 20
	As any comer I have looked on yet
	For my affection.
MOROCCO	Even for that I thank you:
	Therefore, I pray you, lead me to the caskets
	To try my fortune. By this scimitar
	That slew the Sophy and a Persian prince 25
	That won three fields of Sultan Solyman,
	I would outstare the sternest eyes that look,
	Outbrave the heart most daring on the earth,
	Pluck the young sucking cubs from the she-bear,
	Yea, mock the lion when he roars for prey, 30
	To win thee, lady. But, alas the while!
	If Hercules and Lichas play at dice
	Which is the better man, the greater throw
	May turn by fortune from the weaker hand:
	So is Alcides beaten by his page; 35
	And so may I, blind fortune leading me,
	Miss that which one unworthier may attain,
	And die with grieving.

Act 2, Scene 2 — Lancelet Faces a Dilemma

PORTIA	You must take your chance,
	And either not attempt to choose at all
	Or swear before you choose, if you choose wrong 40
	Never to speak to lady afterward
	In way of marriage: therefore be advised.
MOROCCO	Nor will not. Come, bring me unto my chance.
PORTIA	First, forward to the temple: after dinner
	Your hazard shall be made.
MOROCCO	Good fortune then! 45
	To make me blest or cursed'st among men.
	Cornets and exeunt

42 'you have been warned'.

Shakespeare's Techniques

The prince doesn't actually take the test of the caskets until Act 2, Scene 7 — the long wait builds suspense.

Lancelet makes up his mind to stop serving Shylock. He tricks his blind father, before telling him about his plan to serve Bassanio instead. Bassanio accepts Lancelet's offer to serve him and agrees to let Gratiano go with him to Belmont.

ACT 2, SCENE 2

VENICE. A STREET.

Enter LANCELET

LANCELET Certainly my conscience will serve me to run from this Jew my master. The fiend is at mine elbow and tempts me saying to me 'Gobbo, Lancelet Gobbo, good Lancelet', or 'Good Gobbo', or 'Good Lancelet Gobbo, use your legs, take the   5 start, run away.' My conscience says 'No; take heed, honest Lancelet; take heed, honest Gobbo', or, as aforesaid, 'Honest Lancelet Gobbo; do not run; scorn running with thy heels.' Well, the most courageous fiend bids me pack: 'Via!' says the   10 fiend; 'Away!' says the fiend; 'For the heavens, rouse up a brave mind,' says the fiend, 'and run.' Well, my conscience, hanging about the neck of my heart, says very wisely to me, 'My honest friend Lancelet, being an honest man's son,' or   15 rather an honest woman's son — for, indeed, my father did something smack, something grow to, he had a kind of taste — well, my conscience says 'Lancelet, budge not.' 'Budge,' says the fiend. 'Budge not,' says my conscience. 'Conscience,'   20 say I, 'you counsel well.' 'Fiend,' say I, 'you counsel well.' To be ruled by my conscience, I should stay with the Jew my master, who, God bless the mark, is a kind of devil; and, to run away from the Jew, I should be ruled by the fiend,   25

1-2 'I'm certain I'll feel guilty if I run away from my Jewish master.'

6-7 'take heed' means 'listen'.

10 'Via!' means 'Away!'

16-18 In other words — 'for my father was known to have cheated on my mother'.

Character — Lancelet

Lancelet's opening speech is rambling and repetitive, which makes him appear uneducated. The audience can tell straight away that he's the clown character.

23-24 'God bless the mark' means 'pardon my language'.

27 'the Jew is the devil in human form'. Lancelet mistakenly says 'incarnation' instead of 'incarnate'.

Character — Old Gobbo

Old Gobbo only appears in this scene and doesn't contribute to the overall plot. His sole purpose is to create humour.

35-38 'Good heavens, it's my father! He doesn't know who I am because he's blind — I'll try to play a little trick on him.'

45 'Good lord, that will be a hard route to follow.'

49 'Watch me make him cry.'

54-55 'Say what you like about his father, we're talking about Lancelet'.

57 'ergo' means 'therefore'.

62-63 'Fates', 'Destinies' and 'the Sisters Three' all refer to the three goddesses who determined the fate of men in Greek and Roman myths.

66-67 'That boy was meant to support me in my old age.'

68-69 'Do I look like a walking stick to you?'

who, saving your reverence, is the devil himself. Certainly the Jew is the very devil incarnation; and, in my conscience, my conscience is but a kind of hard conscience, to offer to counsel me to stay with the Jew. The fiend gives the more friendly counsel: I will run, fiend; my heels are at your command; I will run. 30

Enter OLD GOBBO, with a basket

OLD GOBBO   Master young man, you, I pray you, which is the way to master Jew's?

LANCELET   *(Aside)* O heavens, this is my true-begotten 35 father! Who, being more than sand-blind, high-gravel blind, knows me not: I will try confusions with him.

OLD GOBBO   Master young gentleman, I pray you, which is the way to master Jew's? 40

LANCELET   Turn up on your right hand at the next turning, but, at the next turning of all, on your left; marry, at the very next turning, turn of no hand, but turn down indirectly to the Jew's house.

OLD GOBBO   By God's sonties, 'twill be a hard way to hit. Can 45 you tell me whether one Lancelet, that dwells with him, dwell with him or no?

LANCELET   Talk you of young Master Lancelet? *(Aside)* Mark me now; now will I raise the waters. Talk you of young Master Lancelet? 50

OLD GOBBO   No master, sir, but a poor man's son: his father, though I say it, is an honest exceeding poor man and, God be thanked, well to live.

LANCELET   Well, let his father be what a' will, we talk of young Master Lancelet. 55

OLD GOBBO   Your worship's friend and Lancelet, sir.

LANCELET   But I pray you, ergo, old man, ergo, I beseech you, talk you of young Master Lancelet?

OLD GOBBO   Of Lancelet, an't please your mastership.

LANCELET   Ergo, Master Lancelet. Talk not of Master 60 Lancelet, father; for the young gentleman, according to Fates and Destinies and such odd sayings, the Sisters Three and such branches of learning, is indeed deceased, or, as you would say in plain terms, gone to heaven. 65

OLD GOBBO   Marry, God forbid! The boy was the very staff of my age, my very prop.

LANCELET   Do I look like a cudgel or a hovel-post, a staff or a prop? Do you know me, father?

OLD GOBBO   Alack the day, I know you not, young gentleman: 70 but, I pray you, tell me, is my boy, God rest his soul, alive or dead?

Act 2, Scene 2

LANCELET	Do you not know me, father?
OLD GOBBO	Alack, sir, I am sand-blind; I know you not.
LANCELET	Nay, indeed, if you had your eyes, you might fail 75 of the knowing me: it is a wise father that knows his own child. Well, old man, I will tell you news of your son. *(He kneels)* Give me your blessing: truth will come to light; murder cannot be hid long; a man's son may, but at the length truth will out. 80
OLD GOBBO	Pray you, sir, stand up: I am sure you are not Lancelet, my boy.
LANCELET	Pray you, let's have no more fooling about it, but give me your blessing: I am Lancelet, your boy that was, your son that is, your child that shall be. 85
OLD GOBBO	I cannot think you are my son.
LANCELET	I know not what I shall think of that: but I am Lancelet, the Jew's man, and I am sure Margery your wife is my mother.
OLD GOBBO	Her name is Margery, indeed: I'll be sworn, if thou 90 be Lancelet, thou art mine own flesh and blood. Lord worshipped might he be! What a beard hast thou got! Thou hast got more hair on thy chin than Dobbin my fill-horse has on his tail.
LANCELET	*(He rises)* It should seem, then, that Dobbin's tail 95 grows backward: I am sure he had more hair of his tail than I have of my face when I last saw him.
OLD GOBBO	Lord, how art thou changed! How dost thou and thy master agree? I have brought him a present. How 'gree you now? 100
LANCELET	Well, well: but, for mine own part, as I have set up my rest to run away, so I will not rest till I have run some ground. My master's a very Jew: give him a present? Give him a halter! I am famished in his service; you may tell every finger I have with 105 my ribs. Father, I am glad you are come: give me your present to one Master Bassanio, who, indeed, gives rare new liveries: if I serve not him, I will run as far as God has any ground. O rare fortune! Here comes the man: to him, father; for 110 I am a Jew, if I serve the Jew any longer.
	Enter BASSANIO, *with* LEONARDO *and other followers*
BASSANIO	*(To a Servant)* You may do so; but let it be so hasted that supper be ready at the farthest by five of the clock. See these letters delivered; put the liveries to making, and desire Gratiano to come 115 anon to my lodging.
	Exit a Servant
LANCELET	To him, father.
OLD GOBBO	*(Comes forward)* God bless your worship!

74 'sand-blind' means 'half-blind'.

Character — Lancelet

Lancelet uses proverbs and sayings to try to seem intelligent. He often gets them wrong, which makes him sound ridiculous.

88 In Elizabethan slang, 'Margery' was another word for a prostitute.

94 'fill-horse' means 'carthorse'.

103-104 'give him a rope to hang himself, not a present!'

Character — Shylock

Even though Lancelet mixes up "finger" and "ribs", his message is clear — Shylock is ungenerous to his servant.

108 'rare new liveries' means 'nice uniforms'.

111 'you may as well call me a Jew if I serve the Jew any longer.'

113 'at the farthest' means 'at the latest'.

116 'anon' means 'shortly'.

Act 2, Scene 2

119 'Thanks! What is it you want?'

Shakespeare's Techniques

Lancelet and Old Gobbo <u>talk over</u> each other and mistake <u>similar-sounding</u> words (e.g. "infection" instead of 'affection'). This creates <u>humour</u>.

127-128 'Lancelet and his master aren't exactly what you would call friends, if you don't mind me saying'.

130-131 Lancelet mistakenly says 'frutify' instead of 'certify'. What he means is 'as my father will tell you'.

138 'One at a time. What do you want?'

Shakespeare's Techniques

The <u>entire scene</u> has been written in <u>prose</u> until now, but Bassanio is set apart as a <u>higher-status</u> character by his use of <u>blank verse</u>.

146-148 The 'old proverb' Lancelet is referring to says 'the grace of God is enough'.

146 'parted' means 'divided'.

152 'guarded' means 'ornamented'.

155 The 'table' is part of the palm.

Shakespeare's Techniques

The humour provided by Lancelet is <u>visual</u> as well as <u>verbal</u>. He makes these <u>nonsense</u> predictions by <u>reading his palm</u> on stage.

164-165 'in the blink of an eye.'

BASSANIO	Gramercy! Wouldst thou aught with me?	
OLD GOBBO	Here's my son, sir, a poor boy —	120
LANCELET	Not a poor boy, sir, but the rich Jew's man; that would, sir, as my father shall specify —	
OLD GOBBO	He hath a great infection, sir, as one would say, to serve —	
LANCELET	Indeed, the short and the long is, I serve the Jew, and have a desire, as my father shall specify —	125
OLD GOBBO	His master and he, saving your worship's reverence, are scarce cater-cousins —	
LANCELET	To be brief, the very truth is that the Jew, having done me wrong, doth cause me, as my father, being, I hope, an old man, shall frutify unto you —	130
OLD GOBBO	I have here a dish of doves that I would bestow upon your worship, and my suit is —	
LANCELET	In very brief, the suit is impertinent to myself, as your worship shall know by this honest old man; and, though I say it, though old man, yet poor man, my father.	135
BASSANIO	One speak for both. What would you?	
LANCELET	Serve you, sir.	
OLD GOBBO	That is the very defect of the matter, sir.	140
BASSANIO	I know thee well; thou hast obtained thy suit: Shylock thy master spoke with me this day, And hath preferred thee, if it be preferment To leave a rich Jew's service, to become The follower of so poor a gentleman.	145
LANCELET	The old proverb is very well parted between my master Shylock and you, sir: you have the grace of God, sir, and he hath enough.	
BASSANIO	Thou speak'st it well. Go, father, with thy son. Take leave of thy old master and inquire My lodging out. *(To a Servant)* Give him a livery More guarded than his fellows': see it done.	150
LANCELET	Father, in. I cannot get a service, no; I have ne'er a tongue in my head. Well, if any man in Italy have a fairer table which doth offer to swear upon a book, I shall have good fortune. Go to, here's a simple line of life: here's a small trifle of wives: alas, fifteen wives is nothing! Eleven widows and nine maids is a simple coming-in for one man: and then to 'scape drowning thrice, and to be in peril of my life with the edge of a feather-bed; here are simple scapes. Well, if Fortune be a woman, she's a good wench for this gear. Father, come; I'll take my leave of the Jew in the twinkling of an eye.	155
		160
		165

Exeunt LANCELET *and* OLD GOBBO

Act 2, Scene 2

BASSANIO	I pray thee, good Leonardo, think on this. *(Gives him a list)* These things being bought and orderly bestowed, Return in haste, for I do feast tonight My best-esteemed acquaintance: hie thee, go.
LEONARDO	My best endeavours shall be done herein.

Enter GRATIANO

GRATIANO	Where is your master?
LEONARDO	Yonder, sir, he walks.

Exit LEONARDO

GRATIANO	Signior Bassanio!
BASSANIO	Gratiano!
GRATIANO	I have a suit to you.
BASSANIO	You have obtained it.
GRATIANO	You must not deny me: I must go with you to Belmont.
BASSANIO	Why then you must. But hear thee, Gratiano; Thou art too wild, too rude and bold of voice; Parts that become thee happily enough And in such eyes as ours appear not faults; But where thou art not known, why, there they show Something too liberal. Pray thee, take pain To allay with some cold drops of modesty Thy skipping spirit, lest through thy wild behaviour I be misconstrued in the place I go to, And lose my hopes.
GRATIANO	Signior Bassanio, hear me: If I do not put on a sober habit, Talk with respect and swear but now and then, Wear prayer-books in my pocket, look demurely, Nay more, while grace is saying, hood mine eyes Thus with my hat, and sigh and say 'Amen', Use all the observance of civility, Like one well studied in a sad ostent To please his grandam, never trust me more.
BASSANIO	Well, we shall see your bearing.
GRATIANO	Nay, but I bar tonight: you shall not gauge me By what we do tonight.
BASSANIO	No, that were pity: I would entreat you rather to put on Your boldest suit of mirth, for we have friends That purpose merriment. But fare you well: I have some business.
GRATIANO	And I must to Lorenzo and the rest: But we will visit you at suppertime.

Exeunt

Line numbers and notes:

170

170 'I'll do my best.'

171 'Yonder' means 'over there'.

175

180

180 'become' means 'suit'.

185

183-187 'Please try to show some restraint. If you don't, your wild behaviour might give the wrong impression and ruin my chances.'

190

195

194

200

Theme — Love

Bassanio accepts Gratiano's request <u>before</u> hearing it. The fact that the Christian characters are <u>willing</u> to do <u>anything</u> for each other shows how <u>close</u> they are.

Theme — Reality and Appearance

Gratiano tells Bassanio he'll <u>behave himself</u> at Belmont, but this means he'll be giving a <u>false impression</u> of his true nature to Portia and Nerissa.

194-195 'Like someone used to putting on a sensible appearance to keep his grandma happy'.

197-198 'you mustn't judge me on how I behave tonight'.

199-201 'I want you in high spirits tonight, because our friends want to have fun.'

Act 2, Scene 3 — Lancelet Says Goodbye

Photographer: Pedro Zepeda

Jessica is <u>sad</u> to see Lancelet <u>leave</u> Shylock's house, but she plans to do <u>the same</u> in the <u>near future</u>. She gives Lancelet a <u>letter</u> to take to Lorenzo.

Character — Jessica

When Jessica describes Shylock's house as "<u>hell</u>", it shows how much she <u>hates</u> living there — this suggests she has a <u>difficult relationship</u> with her <u>father</u>.

3 'Helped to ease the boredom.'

10 'My tears express my feelings.'

Theme — Prejudice

Lancelet says that Jessica <u>can't</u> be a <u>Jew's daughter</u>, because she's so "<u>beautiful</u>" and "<u>sweet</u>". Comments like this one reflect how widespread <u>anti-Semitism</u> was in the 16th century.

13-14 'it isn't very manly to cry'.

16 'heinous' means 'wicked'.

18-19 'I may be his daughter by blood, but my behaviour is completely different to his.'

ACT 2, SCENE 3

VENICE. A ROOM IN SHYLOCK'S HOUSE.

Enter JESSICA *and* LANCELET

JESSICA   I am sorry thou wilt leave my father so:
Our house is hell, and thou, a merry devil,
Didst rob it of some taste of tediousness.
But fare thee well. There is a ducat for thee:
And, Lancelet, soon at supper shalt thou see   5
Lorenzo, who is thy new master's guest:
Give him this letter. Do it secretly;
And so farewell: I would not have my father
See me in talk with thee.

LANCELET   Adieu! Tears exhibit my tongue. Most beautiful   10
pagan, most sweet Jew! If a Christian did not
play the knave and get thee, I am much deceived.
But, adieu: these foolish drops do something
drown my manly spirit: adieu.

JESSICA   Farewell, good Lancelet.   15

Exit LANCELET

Alack, what heinous sin is it in me
To be ashamed to be my father's child!
But though I am a daughter to his blood,
I am not to his manners. O Lorenzo,
If thou keep promise, I shall end this strife,   20
Become a Christian and thy loving wife.

Exit

Shakespeare's Techniques — Structure

Structure has a <u>significant impact</u> on the <u>pace</u>, <u>mood</u> and <u>atmosphere</u> of the play. Act 1 contains three <u>fairly long scenes</u>, but Act 2 is made up of nine <u>shorter scenes</u>. This gives the audience the impression that the <u>action</u> is gradually <u>speeding up</u>.

During Act 2, the play also jumps <u>regularly</u> between <u>different plots</u> and <u>locations</u>. This <u>builds tension</u> by making the audience wait for each <u>plot line</u> to <u>resume</u>.

Act 2, Scene 4 — Lorenzo Reads the Escape Plan

Lorenzo receives <u>Jessica's letter</u> — he finds out Jessica plans to escape <u>that night</u> by <u>disguising herself</u> as his <u>torchbearer</u>.

Photographer: Pedro Zepeda

ACT 2, SCENE 4

VENICE. A STREET.

Enter GRATIANO, LORENZO, SALERIO *and* SOLANIO

LORENZO	Nay, we will slink away in suppertime,	
	Disguise us at my lodging and return,	
	All in an hour.	
GRATIANO	We have not made good preparation.	
SALERIO	We have not spoke us yet of torchbearers.	5
SOLANIO	'Tis vile, unless it may be quaintly ordered,	
	And better in my mind not undertook.	
LORENZO	'Tis now but four o'clock: we have two hours	
	To furnish us.	

Enter LANCELET, *with a letter*

	Friend Lancelet, what's the news?	10
LANCELET	*(Gives him the letter)* An it shall please you to break up this, shall it seem to signify.	
LORENZO	I know the hand: in faith, 'tis a fair hand;	
	And whiter than the paper it writ on	
	Is the fair hand that writ.	
GRATIANO	Love-news, in faith.	15
LANCELET	*(Begins to leave)* By your leave, sir.	
LORENZO	Whither goest thou?	
LANCELET	Marry, sir, to bid my old master the Jew to sup tonight with my new master the Christian.	
LORENZO	Hold here, take this. *(Gives money)* Tell gentle Jessica	20
	I will not fail her; speak it privately.	
	Go, gentlemen.	

Exit LANCELET

	Will you prepare you for this masque tonight?	
	I am provided of a torchbearer.	
SOLANIO	Ay, marry, I'll be gone about it straight.	25
SOLANIO	And so will I.	
LORENZO	Meet me and Gratiano	
	At Gratiano's lodging some hour hence.	
SALERIO	'Tis good we do so.	

Exeunt SALERIO *and* SOLANIO

GRATIANO	Was not that letter from fair Jessica?	

---

1 'slink' means 'sneak'.

6-7 'It'll go wrong if we don't plan it out properly. We would be better off not doing it at all.'

9 'To prepare ourselves'.

11-12 'You'll find out if you open this letter.'

Character — Lorenzo

Lorenzo <u>instantly</u> recognises Jessica's <u>writing</u> and says it's "<u>fair</u>" (beautiful). This hints at the <u>strength</u> of his <u>romantic feelings</u> for her.

17 'Where are you going?'

18 'sup' means 'have supper'.

23 In the 16th century, a 'masque' was a popular form of entertainment involving lots of music and dancing.

27 'in about an hour'.

Act Two

Act 2, Scene 5 — Shylock is Oblivious

30 'I must tell you everything.'

34-35 'If her father gets into heaven, he'll have his daughter to thank for it'.

Theme — Prejudice

Lorenzo isn't <u>accepting</u> of Jessica's background — he <u>loves</u> Jessica <u>in spite</u> of it. When he calls Shylock a "<u>faithless Jew</u>", he shows that he too is <u>prejudiced</u>.

LORENZO	I must needs tell thee all. She hath directed	30
	How I shall take her from her father's house,	
	What gold and jewels she is furnished with,	
	What page's suit she hath in readiness.	
	If e'er the Jew her father come to heaven,	
	It will be for his gentle daughter's sake:	35
	And never dare misfortune cross her foot,	
	Unless she do it under this excuse,	
	That she is issue to a faithless Jew.	
	Come, go with me; *(Gives the letter)*	
	peruse this as thou goest:	
	Fair Jessica shall be my torchbearer.	40
	Exeunt	

After some <u>hesitation</u>, Shylock <u>accepts</u> an <u>invitation</u> to dine with Bassanio. <u>Unaware</u> that Jessica plans to <u>run away</u>, he leaves her <u>in charge</u> of his <u>house</u>.

ACT 2, SCENE 5

3 'gormandise' means 'overeat'.

5 'rend apparel out' means 'wear all your clothes out'.

9-10 'You always liked telling me that I couldn't do anything without being told to do it first.'

13 'wherefore' means 'why'.

16 'prodigal' means 'wasteful'.

Shakespeare's Techniques

Shylock <u>senses</u> something <u>bad</u> is going to <u>happen</u>, but he <u>doesn't know</u> what it is. The <u>audience</u>, on the other hand, <u>knows</u> what Jessica is planning. This creates <u>dramatic irony</u> (see p.5).

19 Dreaming of money bags used to be seen as a sign of bad luck.

	VENICE. SHYLOCK'S HOUSE.	
	Enter SHYLOCK *and* LANCELET	
SHYLOCK	Well, thou shalt see, thy eyes shall be thy judge,	
	The difference of old Shylock and Bassanio: —	
	What, Jessica! — Thou shalt not gormandise,	
	As thou hast done with me: — What, Jessica! —	
	And sleep and snore, and rend apparel out; —	5
	Why, Jessica, I say!	
LANCELET	Why, Jessica!	
SHYLOCK	Who bids thee call? I do not bid thee call.	
LANCELET	Your worship was wont to tell me that	
	I could do nothing without bidding.	10
	Enter JESSICA	
JESSICA	Call you? What is your will?	
SHYLOCK	I am bid forth to supper, Jessica:	
	There are my keys. But wherefore should I go?	
	I am not bid for love; they flatter me:	
	But yet I'll go in hate, to feed upon	15
	The prodigal Christian. Jessica, my girl,	
	Look to my house. I am right loath to go:	
	There is some ill a-brewing towards my rest,	
	For I did dream of money-bags tonight.	
LANCELET	I beseech you, sir, go: my young master doth	20
	expect your reproach.	

Act Two

Act 2, Scene 5

SHYLOCK	So do I his.
LANCELET	An they have conspired together, I will not say you shall see a masque; but if you do, then it was not for nothing that my nose fell a-bleeding on 25 Black Monday last at six o'clock i' the morning, falling out that year on Ash Wednesday was four year, in the afternoon.
SHYLOCK	What, are there masques? Hear you me, Jessica: Lock up my doors; and when you hear the drum 30 And the vile squealing of the wry-necked fife, Clamber not you up to the casements then, Nor thrust your head into the public street To gaze on Christian fools with varnished faces, But stop my house's ears, I mean my casements: 35 Let not the sound of shallow foppery enter My sober house. By Jacob's staff, I swear, I have no mind of feasting forth tonight: But I will go. Go you before me, sirrah; Say I will come. 40
LANCELET	I will go before, sir. *(Aside to Jessica)* Mistress, look out at window, for all this, there will come a Christian by, will be worth a Jewess' eye.
	Exit LANCELET
SHYLOCK	What says that fool of Hagar's offspring, ha?
JESSICA	His words were 'Farewell mistress', nothing else. 45
SHYLOCK	The patch is kind enough, but a huge feeder; Snail-slow in profit, and he sleeps by day More than the wild-cat: drones hive not with me; Therefore I part with him, and part with him To one that would have him help to waste 50 His borrowed purse. Well, Jessica, go in; Perhaps I will return immediately: Do as I bid you; shut doors after you: Fast bind, fast find; A proverb never stale in thrifty mind. 55
	Exit SHYLOCK
JESSICA	Farewell; and if my fortune be not crost, I have a father, you a daughter, lost.
	Exit JESSICA

24-28 Here, Lancelet is mocking Shylock's superstitions by coming up with a list of meaningless omens.

31 A 'fife' is a high-pitched instrument, like a small flute.

32 'casements' means 'windows'.

Shakespeare's Techniques

Shylock uses personification to describe his house. He's desperate to shield its "ears" in case the masque disturbs its serious atmosphere.

36 'foppery' means 'foolishness'.

38 'I'm not in the mood for going out and feasting tonight'.

43 'worth keeping an eye out for'.

44 In the Bible, Hagar and her son were cast out by the Jewish community. Shylock is pointing out that Lancelet isn't Jewish.

46 'patch' means 'fool'.

48 'I won't put up with lazy people ('drones') in my house'.

54 'Keep your possessions safe and you'll be able to find them quickly'.

Shakespeare's Techniques

The play doesn't contain much rhymed verse, so this rhyming couplet stands out. It emphasises Jessica's desire to get away and her cruelty towards Shylock.

Context — Jews in 16th-century Venice

Jessica's shame about her Jewish identity and desire to convert to Christianity could be a consequence of the way Jews were treated in 16th-century Venice:

- Jews weren't allowed to be citizens. They couldn't own land and were forced to live in a separate part of the city. Jessica might want to avoid the stigma and shame that was associated with Jews at the time.

- Marriage between Jews and Christians was forbidden. In order to marry Lorenzo, Jessica has to convert to Christianity first. This makes the audience question if love is her only motivation for marriage.

Act 2, Scene 6 — The Escape is a Success

Photographer: Pedro Zepeda

Lorenzo is <u>late</u> to arrive, but Jessica's <u>escape</u> goes <u>smoothly</u> and she <u>steals</u> a <u>significant amount</u> of Shylock's <u>money</u> as she leaves. Gratiano finds out that Bassanio is <u>leaving</u> for <u>Belmont</u>.

ACT 2, SCENE 6

VENICE. OUTSIDE SHYLOCK'S HOUSE.

Enter GRATIANO and SALERIO, masked

1-2 'This is the roof Lorenzo told us to wait for him under.'

GRATIANO	This is the penthouse under which Lorenzo Desired us to make stand.
SALERIO	His hour is almost past.
GRATIANO	And it is marvel he out-dwells his hour, For lovers ever run before the clock. 5

4-5 'I'm surprised he's late — lovers are always early.'

6-8 'Lovers are ten times more keen on pursuing new love than they are on being faithful to their partners!'

SALERIO	O, ten times faster Venus' pigeons fly To seal love's bonds new-made, than they are wont To keep obligèd faith unforfeited!

Theme — Love

Gratiano uses a <u>wide range</u> of <u>images</u> (lines 9-20) to illustrate the <u>same message</u> — love is far <u>less exciting</u> once it has been <u>achieved</u>.

GRATIANO	That ever holds: who riseth from a feast With that keen appetite that he sits down? 10 Where is the horse that doth untread again His tedious measures with the unbated fire That he did pace them first? All things that are, Are with more spirit chasèd than enjoyed. How like a younker or a prodigal 15 The scarfèd bark puts from her native bay, Hugged and embracèd by the strumpet wind! How like the prodigal doth she return, With over-weathered ribs and ragged sails, Lean, rent and beggared by the strumpet wind! 20

15-17 'It's like when a richly decorated ship sets sail with the enthusiasm of a young man, carried by the wind.'

20 'Destroyed by the same wind that carried her away!'

Enter LORENZO

22 'sorry to keep you waiting'.

24-25 'I'll wait as long for you if you ever want to steal a wife.'

SALERIO	Here comes Lorenzo: more of this hereafter.
LORENZO	Sweet friends, your patience for my long abode; Not I, but my affairs, have made you wait: When you shall please to play the thieves for wives, I'll watch as long for you then. Approach; 25 Here dwells my father Jew. Ho! Who's within?

Enter JESSICA, above, in boy's clothes

28 'Although I'm sure I recognise your voice.'

JESSICA	Who are you? Tell me, for more certainty, Albeit I'll swear that I do know your tongue.
LORENZO	Lorenzo, and thy love.
JESSICA	Lorenzo, certain, and my love indeed, 30 For who love I so much? And now who knows But you, Lorenzo, whether I am yours?
LORENZO	Heaven and thy thoughts are witness that thou art.

33 'Deep down, you know that you're mine.'

31

Act 2, Scene 6

JESSICA	Here, catch this casket; it is worth the pains.	
	I am glad 'tis night, you do not look on me,	35
	For I am much ashamed of my exchange:	
	But love is blind and lovers cannot see	
	The pretty follies that themselves commit;	
	For if they could, Cupid himself would blush	
	To see me thus transformèd to a boy.	40
LORENZO	Descend, for you must be my torchbearer.	
JESSICA	What, must I hold a candle to my shames?	
	They in themselves, good-sooth, are too too light.	
	Why, 'tis an office of discovery, love;	
	And I should be obscured.	
LORENZO	So are you, sweet,	45
	Even in the lovely garnish of a boy.	
	But come at once;	
	For the close night doth play the runaway,	
	And we are stayed for at Bassanio's feast.	
JESSICA	I will make fast the doors, and gild myself	50
	With some more ducats, and be with you straight.	

Exit above

GRATIANO	Now, by my hood, a Gentile and no Jew.	
LORENZO	Beshrew me but I love her heartily;	
	For she is wise, if I can judge of her,	
	And fair she is, if that mine eyes be true,	55
	And true she is, as she hath proved herself,	
	And therefore, like herself, wise, fair and true,	
	Shall she be placèd in my constant soul.	

Enter JESSICA, below

	What, art thou come? On, gentlemen; away!	
	Our masquing mates by this time for us stay.	60

Exeunt LORENZO, JESSICA and SALERIO

Enter ANTONIO

ANTONIO	Who's there?	
GRATIANO	Signior Antonio!	
ANTONIO	Fie, fie, Gratiano! Where are all the rest?	
	'Tis nine o'clock: our friends all stay for you.	
	No masque tonight: the wind is come about;	65
	Bassanio presently will go aboard:	
	I have sent twenty out to seek for you.	
GRATIANO	I am glad on't: I desire no more delight	
	Than to be under sail and gone tonight.	

Exeunt

---

36 'exchange' means 'disguise'.

37-38 'Lovers can't see the silly things that love makes them do'.

39 Cupid was the god of love and desire in Roman mythology.

43 'They're obvious enough as it is.'

44-45 'it's a torchbearer's job to light things up, but I should stay hidden.'

46 'In a boy's clothing'.

48 'Because the darkness is slipping away from us'.

Theme — Wealth

Jessica's theft introduces the possibility that Lorenzo is marrying her for money, but Lorenzo goes on to praise her wisdom and beauty. This suggests he's truly in love with Jessica.

60 'Our friends will be waiting for us at the masque by now.'

Shakespeare's Techniques

The urgency in Antonio's voice builds anticipation, especially as there are lots of references to time in his speech.

65-66 'the winds have changed and Bassanio is about to set sail'.

Act Two

Act 2, Scene 7 — Morocco Takes the Casket Test

© Donald Cooper/photostage

The Prince of Morocco is shown the <u>three caskets</u>. After taking a <u>long time</u> to decide, he chooses the <u>gold</u> one and <u>leaves</u> Belmont <u>empty-handed</u>.

ACT 2, SCENE 7

BELMONT. A ROOM IN PORTIA'S HOUSE.

Flourish of cornets. Enter PORTIA,
with the PRINCE OF MOROCCO *and their trains.*

1 'discover' means 'show'.

PORTIA   Go draw aside the curtains and discover
The several caskets to this noble prince.
(The curtains are opened) Now make your choice.

MOROCCO   The first, of gold, who this inscription bears,
"Who chooseth me shall gain what many men
                 desire."   5
The second, silver, which this promise carries,
"Who chooseth me shall get as much as he
                 deserves."
This third, dull lead, with warning all as blunt,
"Who chooseth me must give and hazard all he
                 hath."
How shall I know if I do choose the right?   10

12 'withal' means 'as well'.

PORTIA   The one of them contains my picture, prince:
If you choose that, then I am yours withal.

MOROCCO   Some god direct my judgment! Let me see;
I will survey the inscriptions back again.
What says this leaden casket?   15
"Who chooseth me must give and hazard all he
                 hath."
Must give: for what? For lead? Hazard for lead?
This casket threatens. Men that hazard all
Do it in hope of fair advantages:
A golden mind stoops not to shows of dross;   20
I'll then nor give nor hazard aught for lead.
What says the silver with her virgin hue?
"Who chooseth me shall get as much as he
                 deserves."
As much as he deserves! Pause there, Morocco,
And weigh thy value with an even hand: 25
If thou be'st rated by thy estimation,
Thou dost deserve enough; and yet enough
May not extend so far as to the lady:
And yet to be afeard of my deserving
Were but a weak disabling of myself.   30
As much as I deserve! Why, that's the lady:
I do in birth deserve her, and in fortunes,
In graces and in qualities of breeding;
But more than these, in love I do deserve.

Shakespeare's Techniques

At this point, the audience <u>doesn't know</u> which <u>casket</u> is the <u>right</u> one. This makes it a <u>tense moment</u> for them.

Context — Religion

In Christianity, there is only <u>one God</u>. This <u>exclamation</u> from the Prince of Morocco suggests that he believes in <u>multiple gods</u>, which marks him as a <u>religious outsider</u>.

18-19 'Men who risk everything expect large rewards as a result'.

20 'dross' means 'rubbish'.

21 'aught' means 'anything'.

29-30 'I'm not doing myself justice by worrying about whether I deserve her or not.'

Act 2, Scene 7

	What if I strayed no further, but chose here?	35
	Let's see once more this saying graved in gold:	
	"Who chooseth me shall gain what many men	
	desire."	
	Why, that's the lady; all the world desires her;	
	From the four corners of the earth they come,	
	To kiss this shrine, this mortal breathing saint:	40
	The Hyrcanian deserts and the vasty wilds	
	Of wide Arabia are as thoroughfares now	
	For princes to come view fair Portia:	
	The watery kingdom, whose ambitious head	
	Spits in the face of heaven, is no bar	45
	To stop the foreign spirits, but they come,	
	As o'er a brook, to see fair Portia.	
	One of these three contains her heavenly picture.	
	Is't like that lead contains her? 'Twere damnation	
	To think so base a thought: it were too gross	50
	To rib her cerecloth in the obscure grave.	
	Or shall I think in silver she's immured,	
	Being ten times undervalued to tried gold?	
	O sinful thought! Never so rich a gem	
	Was set in worse than gold. They have in England	55
	A coin that bears the figure of an angel	
	Stamped in gold, but that's insculped upon;	
	But here an angel in a golden bed	
	Lies all within. Deliver me the key:	
	Here do I choose, and thrive I as I may!	60
PORTIA	There, take it, prince; and if my form lie there,	
	Then I am yours. *(He unlocks the golden casket)*	
MOROCCO	O hell! What have we here?	
	A carrion Death, within whose empty eye	
	There is a written scroll! I'll read the writing.	
	(Reads) "All that glitters is not gold;	65
	Often have you heard that told:	
	Many a man his life hath sold	
	But my outside to behold:	
	Gilded tombs do worms enfold.	
	Had you been as wise as bold,	70
	Young in limbs, in judgment old,	
	Your answer had not been inscrolled:	
	Fare you well; your suit is cold."	
	Cold, indeed; and labour lost:	
	Then, farewell, heat, and welcome, frost!	75
	Portia, adieu. I have too grieved a heart	
	To take a tedious leave: thus losers part.	

Exit MOROCCO with his train. Flourish of cornets.

PORTIA	A gentle riddance. Draw the curtains, go.	
	Let all of his complexion choose me so.	

Exeunt

36 'graved' means 'engraved'.

Character — Portia

The prince isn't the first to say that suitors come from all over to woo Portia — Bassanio does it in Act 1, Scene 1. This makes her seem especially desirable.

41-43 'Suitors are even crossing the Hyrcanian deserts and Arabian wilderness to see beautiful Portia'. (Hyrcania was in modern-day Iran).

51 'enclose her burial cloth'.

54-55 'A jewel as beautiful as her has never been fixed in anything other than gold.'

Shakespeare's Techniques

The prince's explanation of his thought process is wordy and full of imagery. Portia's responses are blunt in comparison, which suggests she's unimpressed by him.

63 'carrion Death' means 'skull'.

Shakespeare's Techniques

The scroll says that even highly-decorated tombs have worms in them. This hints that the prince failed the test because he was too easily taken in by the casket's appearance.

72 'inscrolled' means 'written on this scroll'.

76-77 'I'm too upset to make a fuss of leaving'.

78-79 'Good riddance. Draw the curtains — I hope everyone with his skin colour chooses the same casket.'

Act 2, Scene 8 — Rumours Are Spreading

© Stewart McPherson

Salerio and Solanio describe <u>Shylock's reaction</u> to <u>Jessica's betrayal</u>. They go on to discuss <u>rumours</u> of a <u>shipwreck</u> in the <u>English Channel</u>.

Characters — Salerio and Solanio

Shakespeare uses Salerio and Solanio as <u>narrative devices</u> — they fill the audience in on events that have happened <u>off stage</u>, which allows the plot to <u>progress</u> more <u>quickly</u>.

4 'The evil Jew (Shylock) complained to the Duke'.

8 A 'gondola' is a long, narrow boat used on canals in Venice.

10 'certified' means 'told'.

12-14 'I've never heard an outburst as confusing as the one Shylock gave in the street'.

Theme — Prejudice

Shakespeare probably meant Solanio's <u>cruel imitation</u> of Shylock to be <u>funny</u>, but it might make a <u>modern audience</u> feel <u>sorry</u> for Shylock <u>instead</u>.

25 'Let's hope that Antonio can repay Shylock on time'.

28 'reasoned' means 'spoke'.

29-31 'an Italian ship full of goods was wrecked in the English Channel'.

Shakespeare's Techniques

The audience hears about the <u>rumours</u> of a <u>shipwreck</u> <u>before Antonio</u>. This is a source of <u>dramatic irony</u>.

ACT 2, SCENE 8

VENICE. A STREET.

Enter SALERIO *and* SOLANIO

SALERIO	Why, man, I saw Bassanio under sail:
	With him is Gratiano gone along;
	And in their ship I am sure Lorenzo is not.
SOLANIO	The villain Jew with outcries raised the duke,
	Who went with him to search Bassanio's ship. 5
SALERIO	He came too late, the ship was under sail:
	But there the duke was given to understand
	That in a gondola were seen together
	Lorenzo and his amorous Jessica:
	Besides, Antonio certified the duke 10
	They were not with Bassanio in his ship.
SOLANIO	I never heard a passion so confused,
	So strange, outrageous, and so variable,
	As the dog Jew did utter in the streets:
	'My daughter! O my ducats! O my daughter! 15
	Fled with a Christian! O my Christian ducats!
	Justice! The law! My ducats, and my daughter!
	A sealèd bag, two sealèd bags of ducats,
	Of double ducats, stolen from me by my daughter!
	And jewels, two stones, two rich and precious 20
	stones,
	Stolen by my daughter! Justice! Find the girl;
	She hath the stones upon her, and the ducats.'
SALERIO	Why, all the boys in Venice follow him,
	Crying, his stones, his daughter, and his ducats.
SOLANIO	Let good Antonio look he keep his day, 25
	Or he shall pay for this.
SALERIO	Marry, well remembered.
	I reasoned with a Frenchman yesterday,
	Who told me, in the narrow seas that part
	The French and English, there miscarried 30
	A vessel of our country richly fraught:
	I thought upon Antonio when he told me;
	And wished in silence that it were not his.
SOLANIO	You were best to tell Antonio what you hear;
	Yet do not suddenly, for it may grieve him. 35
SALERIO	A kinder gentleman treads not the earth.
	I saw Bassanio and Antonio part:
	Bassanio told him he would make some speed

Act 2, Scene 9 — Aragon Takes the Casket Test

Of his return: he answered, 'Do not so;
Slubber not business for my sake, Bassanio   40
But stay the very riping of the time;
And for the Jew's bond which he hath of me,
Let it not enter in your mind of love:
Be merry, and employ your chiefest thoughts
To courtship and such fair ostents of love   45
As shall conveniently become you there.'
And even there, his eye being big with tears,
Turning his face, he put his hand behind him,
And with affection wondrous sensible
He wrung Bassanio's hand; and so they parted.   50

SOLANIO   I think he only loves the world for him.
I pray thee, let us go and find him out
And quicken his embracèd heaviness
With some delight or other.

SALERIO   Do we so.

Exeunt

40-41 'Don't rush things for my sake, Bassanio — take all the time that you need'.

45 'ostents' means 'displays'.

Character — Antonio

Here, Salerio makes Antonio seem particularly kind. Antonio is often praised highly by the Christians — this shows he's generally well-liked.

49 'with affection wondrous sensible' means 'affectionately'.

51 In other words — 'he only loves life because of Bassanio.'

53 'quicken his embracèd heaviness' means 'cheer him up'.

The Prince of Aragon chooses the silver casket and fails the test.
Portia and Nerissa are told that another suitor has arrived at Belmont.

ACT 2, SCENE 9

BELMONT. A ROOM IN PORTIA'S HOUSE.

Enter NERISSA *with a Servitor*

NERISSA   Quick, quick, I pray thee; draw the curtain straight:
(The Servitor pulls back the curtains)
The Prince of Aragon hath ta'en his oath,
And comes to his election presently.

Flourish of cornets. Enter the PRINCE OF ARAGON,
PORTIA *and their trains.*

PORTIA   Behold, there stand the caskets, noble prince:
If you choose that wherein I am contained,   5
Straight shall our nuptial rites be solemnized:
But if you fail, without more speech, my lord,
You must be gone from hence immediately.

ARAGON   I am enjoined by oath to observe three things:
First, never to unfold to any one   10
Which casket 'twas I chose; next, if I fail
Of the right casket, never in my life
To woo a maid in way of marriage. Lastly,
If I do fail in fortune of my choice,
Immediately to leave you and be gone.   15

2 Aragon was a kingdom in the north-east of Spain.

6 'We'll be married straight away'.

10 'unfold' means 'reveal'.

Shakespeare's Techniques

The consequences of failing the casket test are harsh for Portia's suitors. This builds suspense, as it makes the stakes seem much higher.

Act Two

Act 2, Scene 9

16 'injunctions' means 'conditions'.

19 'base' means 'inferior'.

21 'You would have to be more attractive for me to risk anything for you.'

27 A 'martlet' is a type of bird that builds its nest on the outer wall of buildings.

Theme — Reality and Appearance

The prince understands that the gold casket is a trap, but his high opinion of himself is his downfall. He automatically assumes that he's worthy of Portia.

37 'cozen' means 'cheat'.

40-42 'If only status, rank and titles went to those who deserved them, not those who gained them using corruption!'

43 'cover' means 'wear a hat'. People were supposed to take off their hats for their superiors.

45-48 'How many so-called nobles would be stripped of their titles and become peasants! And how many peasants would be granted nobility!'

50 'I know what I deserve.'

54 'schedule' means 'scroll'.

Character — The Prince of Aragon

Aragon's shocked reaction to failing the test makes him seem arrogant. These exclamations and questions suggest that he felt entitled to marry Portia.

PORTIA To these injunctions every one doth swear
That comes to hazard for my worthless self.

ARAGON And so have I addressed me. Fortune now
To my heart's hope! Gold; silver; and base lead.
"Who chooseth me must give and hazard all he   20
hath."
You shall look fairer, ere I give or hazard.
What says the golden chest? Ha! Let me see:
"Who chooseth me shall gain what many men
desire."
What many men desire! That 'many' may be meant
By the fool multitude, that choose by show,   25
Not learning more than the fond eye doth teach;
Which pries not to the interior, but, like the martlet,
Builds in the weather on the outward wall,
Even in the force and road of casualty.
I will not choose what many men desire,   30
Because I will not jump with common spirits
And rank me with the barbarous multitudes.
Why, then to thee, thou silver treasure-house;
Tell me once more what title thou dost bear:
"Who chooseth me shall get as much as he   35
deserves."
And well said too; for who shall go about
To cozen fortune and be honourable
Without the stamp of merit? Let none presume
To wear an undeservèd dignity.
O, that estates, degrees and offices   40
Were not derived corruptly, and that clear honour
Were purchased by the merit of the wearer!
How many then should cover that stand bare!
How many be commanded that command!
How much low peasantry would then be gleaned   45
From the true seed of honour! And how much
honour
Picked from the chaff and ruin of the times
To be new-varnished! Well, but to my choice:
"Who chooseth me shall get as much as he
deserves."
I will assume desert. Give me a key for this,   50
And instantly unlock my fortunes here.
(Opens the silver casket)

PORTIA Too long a pause for that which you find there.

ARAGON What's here? The portrait of a blinking idiot,
Presenting me a schedule! I will read it.
How much unlike art thou to Portia!   55
How much unlike my hopes and my deservings!
"Who chooseth me shall have as much as he
deserves."
Did I deserve no more than a fool's head?
Is that my prize? Are my deserts no better?

Act 2, Scene 9

PORTIA	To offend, and judge, are distinct offices	60
	And of opposèd natures.	
ARAGON	What is here?	
	(Reads) "The fire seven times tried this:	
	Seven times tried that judgment is,	
	That did never choose amiss.	
	Some there be that shadows kiss;	65
	Such have but a shadow's bliss:	
	There be fools alive, iwis,	
	Silvered o'er; and so was this.	
	Take what wife you will to bed,	
	I will ever be your head:	70
	So be gone: you are sped."	
	Still more fool I shall appear	
	By the time I linger here	
	With one fool's head I came to woo,	
	But I go away with two.	75
	Sweet, adieu. I'll keep my oath,	
	Patiently to bear my wroth.	
	Exit ARAGON with his train	
PORTIA	Thus hath the candle singed the moth.	
	O, these deliberate fools! When they do choose,	
	They have the wisdom by their wit to lose.	80
NERISSA	The ancient saying is no heresy,	
	Hanging and wiving goes by destiny.	
PORTIA	Come, draw the curtain, Nerissa.	
	Enter Messenger	
MESSENGER	Where is my lady?	
PORTIA	Here: what would my lord?	
MESSENGER	Madam, there is alighted at your gate	85
	A young Venetian, one that comes before	
	To signify the approaching of his lord;	
	From whom he bringeth sensible regreets,	
	To wit, besides commends and courteous breath,	
	Gifts of rich value. Yet I have not seen	90
	So likely an ambassador of love:	
	A day in April never came so sweet,	
	To show how costly summer was at hand,	
	As this fore-spurrer comes before his lord.	
PORTIA	No more, I pray thee: I am half afeard	95
	Thou wilt say anon he is some kin to thee,	
	Thou spend'st such high-day wit in praising him.	
	Come, come, Nerissa; for I long to see	
	Quick Cupid's post that comes so mannerly.	
NERISSA	Bassanio, lord Love, if thy will it be!	100
	Exeunt	

60-61 In other words — 'Who am I to judge what you deserve? I wouldn't want to offend you.'

65 'shadows' means 'reflections'.

65-66 'Those who obsess over their reflection in the mirror will never experience true happiness'.

67 'iwis' means 'certainly'.

72-73 'The longer I stay, the more foolish I'll seem'.

Character — Portia

Portia's reaction shows that she has a harsh side to her character — she dismisses the prince with a metaphor describing him as a "moth".

79-80 'These fools are only good for one thing — losing.'

82 'Only fate decides when we die and who we marry.'

85 'alighted' means 'arrived'.

88 'sensible regreets' means 'gifts'.

Shakespeare's Techniques

The "young Venetian" at the gate is described as a spring day announcing the coming of "summer" (Bassanio). This makes Bassanio's arrival seem like a joyful occasion.

96-97 'Next you'll be telling me you're related to him, what with how much you're praising him.'

99 'mannerly' means 'courteously'.

Act Two — Practice Questions

Quick Questions

1) What is a *"Flourish of cornets"*?

2) Who does Lancelet serve...
   a) ... at the start of Act 2?   b) ... by the end of Act 2?

3) What does Jessica refer to as "hell" in Act 2, Scene 3?

4) How does Lorenzo find out about Jessica's escape plan?

5) In Act 2, Scene 5, who does Shylock describe as "The prodigal Christian"?

6) Why don't the Christians go to the masque at the end of Act 2, Scene 6?

7) What two items does the Prince of Morocco find inside the gold casket?

8) What bad news do Salerio and Solanio discuss in Act 2, Scene 8?

9) Why does the Prince of Aragon choose the silver casket?

In-depth Questions

1) How does Shakespeare make it clear that Lancelet is the clown character?
   Use quotes to support your answer.

2) Why do you think comic scenes like Act 2, Scene 2 are so important to the play?

3) Reread Act 2, Scene 3. Rewrite this scene in modern English.

4) Explain how Shakespeare gives Shylock's house a gloomy atmosphere.

5) How does Shakespeare present Lorenzo and Jessica's relationship in Act 2, Scene 6?

6) Discuss Salerio and Solanio's role as narrative devices in the play so far.

7) How might the way Shylock is treated in Act 2 change the audience's view of him?

8) When the princes fail the casket test, what do Portia's reactions reveal about her character?

9) Imagine you're a costume designer for a production of *The Merchant of Venice*.
   Describe what clothes you'd give to the two princes and explain your choices.

Act 3, Scene 1 — Shylock Loses His Temper

Shylock <u>accuses</u> Salerio and Solanio of <u>playing a part</u> in <u>Jessica's escape</u>. He's more <u>determined</u> than ever to take <u>revenge</u> on Antonio, and <u>justifies</u> taking a pound of his flesh in an <u>angry outburst</u>. Shylock isn't the only one with <u>problems</u>, though — Tubal <u>reveals</u> that Antonio has <u>lost a ship</u>.

© Donald Cooper/photostage

ACT 3, SCENE 1

VENICE. A STREET.

Enter SOLANIO *and* SALERIO

SOLANIO   Now, what news on the Rialto?

SALERIO   Why, yet it lives there unchecked that Antonio hath a ship of rich lading wrecked on the narrow seas; the Goodwins, I think they call the place; a very dangerous flat and fatal, where the carcasses   5 of many a tall ship lie buried, as they say, if my gossip report be an honest woman of her word.

SOLANIO   I would she were as lying a gossip in that as ever knapped ginger or made her neighbours believe she wept for the death of a third husband. But it   10 is true, without any slips of prolixity or crossing the plain highway of talk, that the good Antonio, the honest Antonio — O that I had a title good enough to keep his name company! —

SALERIO   Come, the full stop.   15

SOLANIO   Ha! What sayest thou? Why, the end is, he hath lost a ship.

SALERIO   I would it might prove the end of his losses.

SOLANIO   Let me say 'Amen' betimes, lest the devil cross my prayer, for here he comes in the likeness of a   20 Jew.

Enter SHYLOCK

How now, Shylock! What news among the merchants?

SHYLOCK   You knew, none so well, none so well as you, of my daughter's flight.   25

SALERIO   That's certain: I, for my part, knew the tailor that made the wings she flew withal.

SOLANIO   And Shylock, for his own part, knew the bird was fledged; and then it is the complexion of them all to leave the dam.   30

SHYLOCK   She is damned for it.

SOLANIO   That's certain, if the devil may be her judge.

SHYLOCK   My own flesh and blood to rebel!

SOLANIO   Out upon it, old carrion! Rebels it at these years?

2-3 'There are still rumours a ship full of goods belonging to Antonio has been wrecked in the Channel'.

8-9 Old women were said to like nibbling on ginger — Solanio is saying that he wishes the woman Salerio spoke to was just gossiping.

11 'slips of prolixity' means 'long-windedness'.

11-12 In other words — 'waffling'.

15 'Come on, get to the point.'

19-20 'I'll say 'Amen' now in case the devil prevents me from praying.'

Shakespeare's Techniques

Jessica's escape is described with an <u>extended metaphor</u> — she's described as a <u>bird</u> flying the <u>nest</u>. Salerio and Solanio are using Shylock's <u>own language</u> to <u>mock him</u>.

29 'fledged' means 'able to fly'.

30 A 'dam' is an animal's mother.

Theme — Prejudice

The <u>Christians</u> often refer to Shylock as the "<u>devil</u>". This <u>recurring image</u> emphasises how <u>evil</u> they think he is.

Act 3, Scene 1

37 'black and white'.

38-39 'red and white wine'.

Shakespeare's Techniques

Shakespeare emphasises the differences between Shylock and Jessica using antithesis.

42 A 'prodigal' is someone who spends their money wastefully.

44 'mart' means 'market'.

45 'was wont to' means 'used to'.

52 'cost me half a million ducats'.

54-55 'turned my friends against me and provoked my enemies'.

57 'dimensions' means 'a body'.

57 'affections' means 'emotions'.

Theme — Prejudice

Shylock speaks passionately and persuasively. His point is that Jews are as human as Christians. His speech reveals that he sees himself as a victim of prejudice.

Theme — Justice and Mercy

Shylock tries to justify taking revenge on Antonio. He thinks it's fair for him to seek revenge, as he says it's what a Christian would do.

69-71 'I'll act with the same cruelty that you've taught me — you may not like it, but I'll do it better than my teachers.'

75-76 'Here comes another Jew — you won't find a third to match these two, unless the devil himself becomes a Jew.'

77 Genoa is an Italian city.

SHYLOCK	I say, my daughter is my flesh and blood.	35
SALERIO	There is more difference between thy flesh and hers than between jet and ivory; more between your bloods than there is between red wine and Rhenish. But tell us, do you hear whether Antonio have had any loss at sea or no?	40
SHYLOCK	There I have another bad match: a bankrupt, a prodigal, who dare scarce show his head on the Rialto; a beggar, that was used to come so smug upon the mart; let him look to his bond: he was wont to call me usurer; let him look to his bond: he was wont to lend money for a Christian courtesy; let him look to his bond.	45
SALERIO	Why, I am sure, if he forfeit, thou wilt not take his flesh: what's that good for?	
SHYLOCK	To bait fish withal: if it will feed nothing else, it will feed my revenge. He hath disgraced me, and hindered me half a million; laughed at my losses, mocked at my gains, scorned my nation, thwarted my bargains, cooled my friends, heated mine enemies; and what's his reason? I am a Jew. Hath not a Jew eyes? Hath not a Jew hands, organs, dimensions, senses, affections, passions? Fed with the same food, hurt with the same weapons, subject to the same diseases, healed by the same means, warmed and cooled by the same winter and summer, as a Christian is? If you prick us, do we not bleed? If you tickle us, do we not laugh? If you poison us, do we not die? And if you wrong us, shall we not revenge? If we are like you in the rest, we will resemble you in that. If a Jew wrong a Christian, what is his humility? Revenge. If a Christian wrong a Jew, what should his sufferance be by Christian example? Why, revenge. The villainy you teach me, I will execute, and it shall go hard but I will better the instruction.	50 / 55 / 60 / 65 / 70

Enter a Servant

SERVANT	Gentlemen, my master Antonio is at his house and desires to speak with you both.	
SALERIO	We have been up and down to seek him.	

Enter TUBAL

SOLANIO	Here comes another of the tribe: a third cannot be matched, unless the devil himself turn Jew.	75

Exeunt SOLANIO, SALERIO and Servant

SHYLOCK	How now, Tubal! What news from Genoa? Hast thou found my daughter?	
TUBAL	I often came where I did hear of her, but cannot find her.	80

Act 3, Scene 1

SHYLOCK	Why, there, there, there, there! A diamond gone, cost me two thousand ducats in Frankfurt! The curse never fell upon our nation till now; I never felt it till now: two thousand ducats in that; and other precious, precious jewels. I would my daughter were dead at my foot, and the jewels in her ear! Would she were hearsed at my foot, and the ducats in her coffin! No news of them? Why, so: and I know not what's spent in the search: why, thou loss upon loss! The thief gone with so much, and so much to find the thief; and no satisfaction, no revenge: nor no ill luck stirring but what lights on my shoulders; no sighs but of my breathing; no tears but of my shedding.
TUBAL	Yes, other men have ill luck too: Antonio, as I heard in Genoa —
SHYLOCK	What, what, what? Ill luck, ill luck?
TUBAL	— hath an argosy cast away, coming from Tripolis.
SHYLOCK	I thank God, I thank God. Is't true, is't true?
TUBAL	I spoke with some of the sailors that escaped the wreck.
SHYLOCK	I thank thee, good Tubal: good news, good news! Ha, ha, heard in Genoa?
TUBAL	Your daughter spent in Genoa, as I heard, in one night fourscore ducats.
SHYLOCK	Thou stickest a dagger in me: I shall never see my gold again: fourscore ducats at a sitting! Fourscore ducats!
TUBAL	There came divers of Antonio's creditors in my company to Venice, that swear he cannot choose but break.
SHYLOCK	I am very glad of it: I'll plague him; I'll torture him. I am glad of it.
TUBAL	One of them showed me a ring that he had of your daughter for a monkey.
SHYLOCK	Out upon her! Thou torturest me, Tubal: it was my turquoise; I had it of Leah when I was a bachelor. I would not have given it for a wilderness of monkeys.
TUBAL	But Antonio is certainly undone.
SHYLOCK	Nay, that's true, that's very true. Go, Tubal, fee me an officer; bespeak him a fortnight before. I will have the heart of him, if he forfeit; for, were he out of Venice, I can make what merchandise I will. Go, go, Tubal, and meet me at our synagogue. Go, good Tubal; at our synagogue, Tubal.

Exeunt separately

85
90
95
100
105
110
115
120
125

---

82 Frankfurt is a German city that used to host a famous jewellery fair.

83 In other words — 'Jewish people'.

87 'hearsed' means 'buried'.

90-91 'The thief stole so much, and I've spent so much trying to find her'.

98 'has had a ship wrecked'.

105 'fourscore' means 'eighty'.

Theme — Wealth

Shylock is more concerned about his wealth than he is about Jessica. This fits with the 16th-century idea that Jews were money-obsessed.

109-111 In other words — 'I met some of Antonio's business associates on the way to Venice, and they said he can't repay you.'

Character — Shylock

Shylock's reaction to losing his ring reveals a human side to his character — its value to him is more sentimental than financial.

117 Leah is Shylock's dead wife.

121-122 'Go, Tubal. Find me an officer (to arrest Antonio) — make sure he's ready two weeks before the loan is due.'

124 'I'd be free to do whatever business I liked.'

125 A 'synagogue' is a Jewish place of worship.

Act 3, Scene 2 — A Double Engagement

© Nigel Norrington / ArenaPAL

Bassanio takes the test of the caskets. He chooses correctly and becomes engaged to Portia. Gratiano and Nerissa also get engaged, but it's not all good news — Antonio writes to say that he has missed the deadline for repaying Shylock. Bassanio prepares to return to Venice immediately.

ACT 3, SCENE 2

BELMONT. A ROOM IN PORTIA'S HOUSE.

Enter BASSANIO, PORTIA, GRATIANO, NERISSA *and Attendants*

1 'tarry' means 'wait'.

3 'forbear' means 'be patient'.

6 'I wouldn't say that if I hated you'.

10-11 'I could tell you the right casket to choose, but that would be breaking the promise I made my father.'

14-15 'Curse your eyes — they've enchanted me and split me in two'.

PORTIA	I pray you, tarry: pause a day or two	
	Before you hazard; for, in choosing wrong,	
	I lose your company: therefore forbear awhile.	
	There's something tells me, but it is not love,	
	I would not lose you; and you know yourself,	5
	Hate counsels not in such a quality.	
	But lest you should not understand me well —	
	And yet a maiden hath no tongue but thought —	
	I would detain you here some month or two	
	Before you venture for me. I could teach you	10
	How to choose right, but I am then forsworn;	
	So will I never be: so may you miss me;	
	But if you do, you'll make me wish a sin,	
	That I had been forsworn. Beshrew your eyes,	
	They have o'erlooked me and divided me;	15
	One half of me is yours, the other half yours,	
	Mine own, I would say; but if mine, then yours,	
	And so all yours. O, these naughty times	
	Put bars between the owners and their rights!	
	And so, though yours, not yours. Prove it so,	20
	Let fortune go to hell for it, not I.	
	I speak too long; but 'tis to peise the time,	
	To eke it and to draw it out in length,	
	To stay you from election.	

Theme — Love

Portia's speech suggests she's completely devoted to Bassanio already. The audience hopes that he succeeds in the casket test so she can marry her love.

22 'peise' means 'weigh down'.

25 'the rack' was a torture device used to force people accused of treason to confess to their crimes.

30-31 'Treason and my love have as much in common as snow and fire'.

33 'enforcèd' means 'under great pressure'.

35 'confess and be hanged' was an old saying used by criminals to justify not admitting to their crimes. Portia alters the saying to suggest that Bassanio should tell the truth.

BASSANIO	Let me choose	
	For as I am, I live upon the rack.	25
PORTIA	Upon the rack, Bassanio! Then confess	
	What treason there is mingled with your love.	
BASSANIO	None but that ugly treason of mistrust,	
	Which makes me fear the enjoying of my love:	
	There may as well be amity and life	30
	'Tween snow and fire, as treason and my love.	
PORTIA	Ay, but I fear you speak upon the rack,	
	Where men enforcèd do speak anything.	
BASSANIO	Promise me life, and I'll confess the truth.	
PORTIA	Well then, confess and live.	
BASSANIO	'Confess and love'	35
	Had been the very sum of my confession:	

Act 3, Scene 2

O happy torment, when my torturer
Doth teach me answers for deliverance!
But let me to my fortune and the caskets.

PORTIA   Away, then! I am locked in one of them: 40
If you do love me, you will find me out.
Nerissa and the rest, stand all aloof.
Let music sound while he doth make his choice;
Then, if he lose, he makes a swan-like end,
Fading in music: that the comparison   45
May stand more proper, my eye shall be the stream
And watery death-bed for him. He may win;
And what is music then? Then music is
Even as the flourish when true subjects bow
To a new-crownèd monarch: such it is   50
As are those dulcet sounds in break of day
That creep into the dreaming bridegroom's ear,
And summon him to marriage. Now he goes,
With no less presence, but with much more love,
Than young Alcides, when he did redeem   55
The virgin tribute paid by howling Troy
To the sea-monster: I stand for sacrifice,
The rest aloof are the Dardanian wives,
With blearèd visages, come forth to view
The issue of the exploit. Go, Hercules!   60
Live thou, I live: with much, much more dismay
I view the fight than thou that makest the fray.

Music, whilst BASSANIO *comments on the caskets to himself*

SINGER   Tell me where is fancy bred,
Or in the heart, or in the head?
How begot, how nourishèd?   65
Reply, reply.
It is engendered in the eyes,
With gazing fed; and fancy dies
In the cradle where it lies.
Let us all ring fancy's knell   70
I'll begin it — Ding, dong, bell.

ALL   Ding, dong, bell.
BASSANIO   So may the outward shows be least themselves:
The world is still deceived with ornament.
In law, what plea so tainted and corrupt,   75
But, being seasoned with a gracious voice,
Obscures the show of evil? In religion,
What damnèd error, but some sober brow
Will bless it and approve it with a text,
Hiding the grossness with fair ornament?   80
There is no vice so simple but assumes
Some mark of virtue on his outward parts:
How many cowards, whose hearts are all as false
As stairs of sand, wear yet upon their chins
The beards of Hercules and frowning Mars;   85
Who, inward searched, have livers white as milk;

37-38 'Torture isn't so bad when my torturer tells me how to get out of it!'

42 'aloof' means 'aside'.

44 'swan-like end' refers to the myth that swans sing as they die.

46-47 'my tears will be the river that carries him to a watery grave'.

51 'dulcet' means 'pleasant'.

51-53 In the 16th century, the groom was traditionally woken up by music on his wedding day.

Character — Portia

Portia compares herself to a princess rescued from a monster by Hercules (see the bottom of p.20). This shows she sees Bassanio's attempt at the test as a chance to avoid a horrible fate.

59 'blearèd' means 'tear-stained'.

61-62 'It's much harder for me to watch than it is for you to decide.'

63 'fancy' means 'desire'.

Shakespeare's Techniques

The first three lines of this song all rhyme with 'lead'. This gives Bassanio a clue about the correct casket.

67 'engendered' means 'produced'.

74 'ornament' means 'appearances'.

Theme — Reality and Appearance

Bassanio's speech is full of examples of how deceptive appearances can be. Here, he points out that criminals tell lies in court to conceal how evil they actually are.

85 In Roman mythology, Mars was the god of war.

86 In other words — 'are cowards'.

Act Three

Act 3, Scene 2

87-88 'And they grow beards to convince others that they're brave.'

89 'it can be bought and sold by the ounce (i.e. like make-up).'

91 'lightest' means 'most foolish'.

92-96 'curly blonde hair that moves playfully in the wind on a beautiful woman is often a wig taken from a dead woman's head'.

97 'guilèd' means 'treacherous'.

101 'gaudy' means 'flashy'.

101-102 In Greek mythology, everything King Midas touched turned to gold, including food.

103-104 'drudge' means 'servant'. Bassanio is saying silver is like a servant, as men trade silver coins.

Character — Bassanio

Bassanio is a risk-taker — he's the only suitor willing to risk everything on the "meagre" (plain) lead casket.

116 'counterfeit' means 'portrait'.

117-119 'Are her eyes moving, or are my eyes playing tricks on me?'

120-121 'only a breath as sweet as hers could part such lovely lips.'

124 'gnats' are small flies.

125-127 'After painting the first eye, I would've thought he'd be too busy staring at it to paint the second one.'

Theme — Love

Bassanio's praise of Portia is excessive. This makes his love seem over the top, which hints that it may not be his only reason for marrying her.

128 'shadow' means 'image'.

130 'substance' means 'reality'.

And these assume but valour's excrement
To render them redoubted. Look on beauty,
And you shall see 'tis purchased by the weight;
Which therein works a miracle in nature, 90
Making them lightest that wear most of it:
So are those crispèd snaky golden locks
Which make such wanton gambols with the wind,
Upon supposèd fairness, often known
To be the dowry of a second head, 95
The skull that bred them in the sepulchre.
Thus ornament is but the guilèd shore
To a most dangerous sea; the beauteous scarf
Veiling an Indian beauty; in a word,
The seeming truth which cunning times put on 100
To entrap the wisest. Therefore, thou gaudy gold,
Hard food for Midas, I will none of thee;
Nor none of thee, thou pale and common drudge
'Tween man and man: but thou, thou meagre lead,
Which rather threatenest than dost promise aught, 105
Thy paleness moves me more than eloquence;
And here choose I; joy be the consequence!

PORTIA   *(Aside)* How all the other passions fleet to air,
As doubtful thoughts, and rash-embraced despair,
And shuddering fear, and green-eyed jealousy! 110
O love, be moderate; allay thy ecstasy,
In measure rein thy joy; scant this excess.
I feel too much thy blessing: make it less,
For fear I surfeit.

BASSANIO   *(Opens the lead casket)* What find I here? 115
Fair Portia's counterfeit! What demi-god
Hath come so near creation? Move these eyes?
Or whether, riding on the balls of mine,
Seem they in motion? Here are severed lips,
Parted with sugar breath: so sweet a bar 120
Should sunder such sweet friends. Here in her
                                                hairs
The painter plays the spider and hath woven
A golden mesh to entrap the hearts of men,
Faster than gnats in cobwebs; but her eyes —
How could he see to do them? Having made one, 125
Methinks it should have power to steal both his
And leave itself unfurnished. Yet look, how far
The substance of my praise doth wrong this
                                                shadow
In underprizing it, so far this shadow
Doth limp behind the substance. Here's the scroll, 130
The continent and summary of my fortune.
(Reads) "You that choose not by the view,
Chance as fair and choose as true!
Since this fortune falls to you,
Be content and seek no new. 135

Act 3, Scene 2

If you be well pleased with this
And hold your fortune for your bliss,
Turn you where your lady is
And claim her with a loving kiss."
A gentle scroll. Fair lady, by your leave; 140
I come by note, to give and to receive.
Like one of two contending in a prize,
That thinks he hath done well in people's eyes,
Hearing applause and universal shout,
Giddy in spirit, still gazing in a doubt 145
Whether these pearls of praise be his or no;
So, thrice fair lady, stand I, even so;
As doubtful whether what I see be true,
Until confirmed, signed, ratified by you.

PORTIA You see me, Lord Bassanio, where I stand, 150
Such as I am: though for myself alone
I would not be ambitious in my wish,
To wish myself much better; yet, for you
I would be trebled twenty times myself;
A thousand times more fair, ten thousand times
                                    more rich; 155
That only to stand high in your account,
I might in virtue, beauties, livings, friends,
Exceed account. But the full sum of me
Is sum of something, which, to term in gross,
Is an unlessoned girl, unschooled, unpractisèd; 160
Happy in this, she is not yet so old
But she may learn. Happier than this,
She is not bred so dull but she can learn;
Happiest of all is that her gentle spirit
Commits itself to yours to be directed, 165
As from her lord, her governor, her king.
Myself and what is mine to you and yours
Is now converted: but now I was the lord
Of this fair mansion, master of my servants,
Queen o'er myself: and even now, but now, 170
This house, these servants and this same myself
Are yours, my lord: I give them with this ring;
Which when you part from, lose, or give away,
Let it presage the ruin of your love
And be my vantage to exclaim on you. 175
(Puts the ring on his finger)

BASSANIO Madam, you have bereft me of all words,
Only my blood speaks to you in my veins;
And there is such confusion in my powers,
As after some oration fairly spoke
By a belovèd prince, there doth appear 180
Among the buzzing pleasèd multitude;
Where every something, being blent together,
Turns to a wild of nothing, save of joy,
Expressed and not expressed. But when this ring

---

141 'by note' means 'with the permission of this note'.

142-146 In other words — 'Like someone who's delighted because he thinks he's won a competition, but isn't sure if the applause is for him or not.'

149 'ratified' means 'approved'.

151-154 'I wouldn't change for my own sake, but I'd make myself infinitely better for you'.

Context — Marriage

Portia's use of business-like language like "rich", "sum" and "account" reflects the fact that marriage was often about securing money and status in the 16th century.

158 'Exceed your expectations'.

159 'to put it briefly'.

161 'Happy' means 'fortunate'.

Shakespeare's Techniques

The ring is a symbol of Bassanio's commitment to Portia. Shakespeare uses it to explore ideas about loyalty after Antonio's trial.

174 'presage' means 'signify'.

175 'And give me the right to be mad at you'.

177 'But my feelings are responding to what you're saying'.

178-184 'The confusion I'm feeling is like the wordless cheering of a crowd after a speech by a well-loved prince.'

Act 3, Scene 2

	Parts from this finger, then parts life from hence:	185
	O, then be bold to say Bassanio's dead!	
NERISSA	My lord and lady, it is now our time,	
	That have stood by and seen our wishes prosper,	
	To cry, good joy: good joy, my lord and lady!	
GRATIANO	My lord Bassanio and my gentle lady,	190
	I wish you all the joy that you can wish;	
	For I am sure you can wish none from me:	
	And when your honours mean to solemnize	
	The bargain of your faith, I do beseech you,	
	Even at that time I may be married too.	195
BASSANIO	With all my heart, so thou canst get a wife.	
GRATIANO	I thank your lordship, you have got me one.	
	My eyes, my lord, can look as swift as yours:	
	You saw the mistress, I beheld the maid;	
	You loved, I loved, for intermission	200
	No more pertains to me, my lord, than you.	
	Your fortune stood upon the casket there,	
	And so did mine too, as the matter falls;	
	For wooing here until I sweat again,	
	And sweating until my very roof was dry	205
	With oaths of love, at last, if promise last,	
	I got a promise of this fair one here	
	To have her love, provided that your fortune	
	Achieved her mistress.	
PORTIA	Is this true, Nerissa?	210
NERISSA	Madam, it is, so you stand pleased withal.	
BASSANIO	And do you, Gratiano, mean good faith?	
GRATIANO	Yes, faith, my lord.	
BASSANIO	Our feast shall be much honoured in your marriage.	
GRATIANO	We'll play with them the first boy for a thousand	215
	ducats.	
NERISSA	What, and stake down?	
GRATIANO	No; we shall ne'er win at that sport, and stake	
	down. But who comes here? Lorenzo and his	
	infidel? What, and my old Venetian friend Salerio?	220

Enter LORENZO, JESSICA *and* SALERIO

BASSANIO	Lorenzo and Salerio, welcome hither;	
	If that the youth of my new interest here	
	Have power to bid you welcome. By your leave,	
	I bid my very friends and countrymen,	
	Sweet Portia, welcome.	225
PORTIA	So do I, my lord. They are entirely welcome.	
LORENZO	I thank your honour. For my part, my lord,	
	My purpose was not to have seen you here;	
	But meeting with Salerio by the way,	
	He did entreat me, past all saying nay,	230
	To come with him along.	

186 'then you can be sure Bassanio is dead!'

193-195 'And when you get married, I hope you'll let me get married at the same time.'

Shakespeare's Techniques

The repetitive structure of these lines reflects the way that Gratiano's actions echo Bassanio's actions here.

200-201 'for I'm no more keen on waiting around than you are'.

205 'the roof of my mouth'.

208-209 'on the condition that you and Portia got engaged first.'

211 'as long as you're OK with it.'

215-216 'I'll bet a thousand ducats that we'll have a son before they do.'

Theme — Prejudice

Jessica is now a Christian, but Gratiano still calls her an "infidel" (non-believer). Marrying Lorenzo doesn't mean that she's accepted by the other Christians.

222-223 'If my new-found authority is great enough to bid you welcome.'

230 'entreat' means 'beg'.

Act 3, Scene 2

SALERIO	I did, my lord;
	And I have reason for it. Signior Antonio
	Commends him to you. *(Gives Bassanio a letter)*
BASSANIO	Ere I ope his letter,
	I pray you, tell me how my good friend doth. 235
SALERIO	Not sick, my lord, unless it be in mind;
	Nor well, unless in mind: his letter there
	Will show you his estate. *(Bassanio opens the letter)*
GRATIANO	Nerissa, cheer yon stranger; bid her welcome.
	Your hand, Salerio: what's the news from Venice? 240
	How doth that royal merchant, good Antonio?
	I know he will be glad of our success;
	We are the Jasons, we have won the fleece.
SALERIO	I would you had won the fleece that he hath lost.
PORTIA	There are some shrewd contents in yon same
	paper, 245
	That steals the colour from Bassanio's cheek:
	Some dear friend dead; else nothing in the world
	Could turn so much the constitution
	Of any constant man. What, worse and worse!
	With leave, Bassanio: I am half yourself, 250
	And I must freely have the half of anything
	That this same paper brings you.
BASSANIO	O sweet Portia,
	Here are a few of the unpleasant'st words
	That ever blotted paper! Gentle lady,
	When I did first impart my love to you, 255
	I freely told you, all the wealth I had
	Ran in my veins, I was a gentleman;
	And then I told you true: and yet, dear lady,
	Rating myself at nothing, you shall see
	How much I was a braggart. When I told you 260
	My state was nothing, I should then have told you
	That I was worse than nothing; for, indeed,
	I have engaged myself to a dear friend,
	Engaged my friend to his mere enemy,
	To feed my means. Here is a letter, lady; 265
	The paper as the body of my friend,
	And every word in it a gaping wound,
	Issuing life-blood. But is it true, Salerio?
	Have all his ventures failed? What, not one hit?
	From Tripolis, from Mexico and England, 270
	From Lisbon, Barbary and India?
	And not one vessel 'scape the dreadful touch
	Of merchant-marring rocks?
SALERIO	Not one, my lord.
	Besides, it should appear, that if he had
	The present money to discharge the Jew, 275
	He would not take it. Never did I know

234 'Ere' means 'before'.

237-238 'his letter here will tell you how he's getting on.'

Shakespeare's Techniques

Shakespeare makes a pun on the similar-sounding words 'fleece' (sheep's wool) and 'fleets' (a group of ships). This draws attention to Antonio's losses.

245-246 'There's something ominous written in that letter that has made Bassanio go pale'.

248 'constitution' means 'mood'.

249 'constant' means 'emotionally stable'.

256-257 'I told you I was poor, but that I had noble blood in my veins'.

260 'braggart' means 'show-off'.

Character — Bassanio

Until now, Bassanio has been hiding his debts from Portia. This shows that he understands appearances can be misleading.

263-265 'I've borrowed money from a dear friend, who borrowed it from his sworn enemy to help me.'

Shakespeare's Techniques

Bassanio uses a metaphor that describes Antonio's words as bleeding wounds. This reminds the audience of the pound of flesh that Shylock is now entitled to.

271 'Barbary' was a 16th-century name for the north coast of Africa.

275 'discharge' means 'repay'.

Act 3, Scene 2

278 'confound' means 'destroy'.

279 'plies' means 'pesters'.

280 'challenges Venice's liberty'. Salerio is saying that denying Shylock his bond would be harmful for Venice.

282-283 'some of the most influential men in the city'.

Character — Shylock

Salerio and Jessica make Shylock sound bloodthirsty. This suggests that there isn't any chance of him showing mercy to Antonio.

295-298 'The most good-natured and generous soul, who is more honourable than any man in Italy.'

Theme — Wealth

Portia's offer to repay the debt to Shylock (and more) makes her seem selfless — it shows that money isn't as important to her as helping Bassanio save his friend.

309 'petty' means 'insignificant'.

312 'maids' means 'virgins'.

315 'As marrying you is expensive, I'll love you even more because of it.'

317-318 'my ships have all been wrecked'.

Shakespeare's Techniques

The tone of Antonio's letter is resigned. This creates a gloomy mood, which contrasts with the joyful mood earlier in the scene.

	A creature, that did bear the shape of man,	
	So keen and greedy to confound a man:	
	He plies the duke at morning and at night,	
	And doth impeach the freedom of the state,	280
	If they deny him justice. Twenty merchants,	
	The duke himself, and the magnificoes	
	Of greatest port, have all persuaded with him;	
	But none can drive him from the envious plea	
	Of forfeiture, of justice and his bond.	285
JESSICA	When I was with him I have heard him swear	
	To Tubal and to Chus, his countrymen,	
	That he would rather have Antonio's flesh	
	Than twenty times the value of the sum	
	That he did owe him: and I know, my lord,	290
	If law, authority and power deny not,	
	It will go hard with poor Antonio.	
PORTIA	Is it your dear friend that is thus in trouble?	
BASSANIO	The dearest friend to me, the kindest man,	
	The best-conditioned and unwearied spirit	295
	In doing courtesies, and one in whom	
	The ancient Roman honour more appears	
	Than any that draws breath in Italy.	
PORTIA	What sum owes he the Jew?	
BASSANIO	For me three thousand ducats.	
PORTIA	What, no more?	300
	Pay him six thousand, and deface the bond;	
	Double six thousand, and then treble that,	
	Before a friend of this description	
	Shall lose a hair through Bassanio's fault.	
	First go with me to church and call me wife,	305
	And then away to Venice to your friend;	
	For never shall you lie by Portia's side	
	With an unquiet soul. You shall have gold	
	To pay the petty debt twenty times over:	
	When it is paid, bring your true friend along.	310
	My maid Nerissa and myself meantime	
	Will live as maids and widows. Come, away!	
	For you shall hence upon your wedding-day:	
	Bid your friends welcome, show a merry cheer:	
	Since you are dear bought, I will love you dear.	315
	But let me hear the letter of your friend.	
BASSANIO	(Reads) "Sweet Bassanio, my ships have all miscarried, my creditors grow cruel, my estate is very low, my bond to the Jew is forfeit; and since in paying it, it is impossible I should live, all debts are cleared between you and I, if I might but see you at my death. Notwithstanding, use your pleasure: if your love do not persuade you to come, let not my letter."	320
PORTIA	O love, dispatch all business, and be gone!	325

Act Three

Act 3, Scene 3 — Shylock Won't Listen to Antonio

| BASSANIO | Since I have your good leave to go away,
I will make haste: but, till I come again,
No bed shall e'er be guilty of my stay,
No rest be interposer 'twixt us twain. |
| | *Exeunt* |

327-329 'I won't sleep or rest until I get back and we're together again.'

Antonio begs Shylock to take pity on him, but Shylock won't listen.
Antonio admits to Solanio that nothing can be done to save him.

© Manuel Harlan

ACT 3, SCENE 3

VENICE. A STREET.

Enter SHYLOCK, SOLANIO, ANTONIO and Jailer

SHYLOCK	Jailer, look to him: tell not me of mercy; This is the fool that lent out money gratis: Jailer, look to him.	
ANTONIO	Hear me yet, good Shylock.	
SHYLOCK	I'll have my bond; speak not against my bond: I have sworn an oath that I will have my bond. Thou calledst me dog before thou hadst a cause; But, since I am a dog, beware my fangs: The duke shall grant me justice. I do wonder, Thou naughty Jailer, that thou art so fond To come abroad with him at his request.	5 10
ANTONIO	I pray thee, hear me speak.	
SHYLOCK	I'll have my bond; I will not hear thee speak: I'll have my bond; and therefore speak no more. I'll not be made a soft and dull-eyed fool, To shake the head, relent, and sigh, and yield To Christian intercessors. Follow not; I'll have no speaking: I will have my bond.	 15
	Exit SHYLOCK	
SOLANIO	It is the most impenetrable cur That ever kept with men.	
ANTONIO	Let him alone: I'll follow him no more with bootless prayers. He seeks my life; his reason well I know: I oft delivered from his forfeitures Many that have at times made moan to me; Therefore he hates me.	20

2 'gratis' means 'without interest'.

10-11 'willing to let him out of jail'.

Shakespeare's Techniques

Shylock's repetition of "I'll have my bond" highlights how determined he is to take revenge on Antonio.

16-17 In other words — 'give in to the Christians who beg for Antonio'.

19-20 'He's the most stubborn dog that ever lived among men.'

21 'bootless' means 'pointless'.

23-24 'I've often given money to people who are in debt to him'.

Act Three

Act 3, Scene 4 — Portia Has a Plan

28 'strangers' means 'foreigners'. This term includes Shylock, as Jews weren't allowed to become citizens.

30 'impeach' means 'discredit'.

Context — Venice

In the 16th century, Venice's law was known for treating foreign traders fairly — this attracted businessmen from all over the world. Denying Shylock his bond would damage this reputation.

Theme — Love

Antonio's only wish before he dies is to see Bassanio. This shows how much their friendship matters to him.

SOLANIO	I am sure the duke	25
	Will never grant this forfeiture to hold.	
ANTONIO	The duke cannot deny the course of law:	
	For the commodity that strangers have	
	With us in Venice, if it be denied,	
	Will much impeach the justice of his state;	30
	Since that the trade and profit of the city	
	Consisteth of all nations. Therefore, go:	
	These griefs and losses have so bated me,	
	That I shall hardly spare a pound of flesh	
	Tomorrow to my bloody creditor.	35
	Well, Jailer, on. Pray God, Bassanio come	
	To see me pay his debt, and then I care not!	
	Exeunt	

Lorenzo praises Portia for agreeing to help Antonio. Portia asks Lorenzo to take care of Belmont, telling him that she and Nerissa are going to wait for their husbands in a nearby monastery. She's lying — when Lorenzo is gone, Portia lets Nerissa in on her plan to follow Bassanio and Gratiano to Venice.

ACT 3, SCENE 4

BELMONT. A ROOM IN PORTIA'S HOUSE.

Enter PORTIA, NERISSA, LORENZO, JESSICA *and* BALTHASAR

2-3 'You have great respect for the divine nature of friendship'.

8-9 'I know you'd be more proud of helping Antonio than you'd be of any ordinary act of generosity.'

11-15 In other words — 'close friends must share many of the same traits and characteristics'.

17 'as Bassanio's closest friend'.

LORENZO	Madam, although I speak it in your presence,	
	You have a noble and a true conceit	
	Of godlike amity; which appears most strongly	
	In bearing thus the absence of your lord.	
	But if you knew to whom you show this honour,	5
	How true a gentleman you send relief,	
	How dear a lover of my lord your husband,	
	I know you would be prouder of the work	
	Than customary bounty can enforce you.	
PORTIA	I never did repent for doing good,	10
	Nor shall not now: for in companions	
	That do converse and waste the time together,	
	Whose souls do bear an equal yoke of love,	
	There must be needs a like proportion	
	Of lineaments, of manners and of spirit;	15
	Which makes me think that this Antonio,	
	Being the bosom lover of my lord,	
	Must needs be like my lord. If it be so,	

Act 3, Scene 4

	How little is the cost I have bestowed	
	In purchasing the semblance of my soul	20
	From out the state of hellish misery!	
	This comes too near the praising of myself;	
	Therefore no more of it: hear other things.	
	Lorenzo, I commit into your hands	
	The husbandry and manage of my house	25
	Until my lord's return: for mine own part,	
	I have toward heaven breathed a secret vow	
	To live in prayer and contemplation,	
	Only attended by Nerissa here,	
	Until her husband and my lord's return:	30
	There is a monastery two miles off;	
	And there will we abide. I do desire you	
	Not to deny this imposition;	
	The which my love and some necessity	
	Now lays upon you.	35
LORENZO	Madam, with all my heart;	
	I shall obey you in all fair commands.	
PORTIA	My people do already know my mind,	
	And will acknowledge you and Jessica	
	In place of Lord Bassanio and myself.	40
	And so farewell, till we shall meet again.	
LORENZO	Fair thoughts and happy hours attend on you!	
JESSICA	I wish your ladyship all heart's content.	
PORTIA	I thank you for your wish, and am well pleased	
	To wish it back on you: fare you well Jessica.	45
	Exeunt JESSICA *and* LORENZO	
	Now, Balthasar,	
	As I have ever found thee honest-true,	
	So let me find thee still. Take this same letter,	
	And use thou all the endeavour of a man	
	In speed to Padua: see thou render this	50
	Into my cousin's hand, Doctor Bellario;	
	And, look, what notes and garments he doth	
	give thee,	
	Bring them, I pray thee, with imagined speed	
	Unto the traject, to the common ferry	
	Which trades to Venice. Waste no time in words,	55
	But get thee gone: I shall be there before thee.	
BALTHASAR	Madam, I go with all convenient speed.	
	Exit BALTHASAR	
PORTIA	Come on, Nerissa; I have work in hand	
	That you yet know not of: we'll see our husbands	
	Before they think of us.	
NERISSA	Shall they see us?	60
PORTIA	They shall, Nerissa; but in such a habit,	
	That they shall think we are accomplishèd	
	With that we lack. I'll hold thee any wager,	

Character — Portia

Portia is lying to Lorenzo — she convinces him that she's going to a monastery, when really she's about to go to Venice. This shows she has a mischievous side.

32-35 'Don't deny this request — I'm asking you because I have to.'

25 'husbandry' means 'care'.

Shakespeare's Techniques

Portia's imperatives give her speech a purposeful tone. They increase the pace of the action by suggesting that urgency is required.

50 Padua is a city near Venice.

51 In the 16th century, 'Doctor' was another word for 'lawyer'.

53 'as quickly as possible'.

54 'traject' means 'ferry'.

Shakespeare's Techniques

Shakespeare structures the play so that the audience doesn't know exactly what Portia is up to until Act 4. This creates anticipation.

61-63 'They'll see us, but our clothes will make them think we're equipped with what we lack (a penis).' Portia is saying that they'll be disguised as men.

Act Three

Act 3, Scene 5 — Lancelet Causes Mischief

64 'accoutred' means 'dressed'.

67-68 'And I'll speak with the breaking voice of a teenage boy'.

69 'frays' means 'fights'.

Character — Portia

Portia makes fun of the way 16th-century men behaved. She can mimic their actions, which might explain why her disguise is so convincing in Act 4.

79 'turn to' means 'become' but also 'make ourselves sexually available to'.

80-81 'What kind of question is that? It's a good thing no one with a dirty mind overheard you!'

82 'device' means 'plan'.

	When we are both accoutred like young men,	
	I'll prove the prettier fellow of the two,	65
	And wear my dagger with the braver grace,	
	And speak between the change of man and boy	
	With a reed voice, and turn two mincing steps	
	Into a manly stride, and speak of frays	
	Like a fine bragging youth, and tell quaint lies,	70
	How honourable ladies sought my love,	
	Which I denying, they fell sick and died;	
	I could not do withal; then I'll repent,	
	And wish for all that, that I had not killed them;	
	And twenty of these puny lies I'll tell,	75
	That men shall swear I have discontinued school	
	Above a twelvemonth. I have within my mind	
	A thousand raw tricks of these bragging Jacks,	
	Which I will practise.	
NERISSA	Why, shall we turn to men?	
PORTIA	Fie, what a question's that,	80
	If thou wert near a lewd interpreter!	
	But come, I'll tell thee all my whole device	
	When I am in my coach, which stays for us	
	At the park gate; and therefore haste away,	
	For we must measure twenty miles today.	85

Exeunt

Lancelet teases Jessica, then he annoys Lorenzo by deliberately misunderstanding his orders. Lorenzo and Jessica discuss Portia.

ACT 3, SCENE 5

1-2 'children are punished for the sins of their fathers'.

Context — Anti-Semitism

Lancelet's belief that Jessica is "damned" for her Jewish origins would have been shared by Shakespeare's audiences. At the time, Christians thought that all Jews went straight to hell.

6-8 'You've only got one hope of salvation, and it's a false one.'

BELMONT. A GARDEN.

Enter LANCELET *and* JESSICA

LANCELET	Yes, truly; for, look you, the sins of the father are to be laid upon the children: therefore, I promise ye, I fear you. I was always plain with you, and so now I speak my agitation of the matter: therefore be of good cheer, for truly I think you are damned. There is but one hope in it that can do you any good; and that is but a kind of bastard hope neither.	5
JESSICA	And what hope is that, I pray thee?	
LANCELET	Marry, you may partly hope that your father got you not, that you are not the Jew's daughter.	10

Act Three

Act 3, Scene 5

JESSICA	That were a kind of bastard hope, indeed: so the sins of my mother should be visited upon me.
LANCELET	Truly then I fear you are damned both by father and mother: thus when I shun Scylla, your father, I fall into Charybdis, your mother: well, you are gone both ways.
JESSICA	I shall be saved by my husband; he hath made me a Christian.
LANCELET	Truly, the more to blame he: we were Christians enow before; e'en as many as could well live, one by another. This making Christians will raise the price of hogs: if we grow all to be pork-eaters, we shall not shortly have a rasher on the coals for money.

Enter LORENZO

JESSICA	I'll tell my husband, Lancelet, what you say: here he comes.
LORENZO	I shall grow jealous of you shortly, Lancelet, if you thus get my wife into corners.
JESSICA	Nay, you need not fear us, Lorenzo: Lancelet and I are out. He tells me flatly, there is no mercy for me in heaven, because I am a Jew's daughter: and he says, you are no good member of the commonwealth, for in converting Jews to Christians, you raise the price of pork.
LORENZO	I shall answer that better to the commonwealth than you can the getting up of the negro's belly: the Moor is with child by you, Lancelet.
LANCELET	It is much that the Moor should be more than reason: but if she be less than an honest woman, she is indeed more than I took her for.
LORENZO	How every fool can play upon the word! I think the best grace of wit will shortly turn into silence, and discourse grow commendable in none only but parrots. Go in, sirrah; bid them prepare for dinner.
LANCELET	That is done, sir; they have all stomachs.
LORENZO	Goodly Lord, what a wit-snapper are you? Then bid them prepare dinner.
LANCELET	That is done too, sir; only 'cover' is the word.
LORENZO	Will you cover then, sir?
LANCELET	Not so, sir, neither; I know my duty.
LORENZO	Yet more quarrelling with occasion! Wilt thou show the whole wealth of thy wit in an instant? I pray thee, understand a plain man in his plain meaning: go to thy fellows; bid them cover the table, serve in the meat, and we will come in to dinner.

12-13 'That really is a false hope, because then I'd be punished for the sins of my mother instead.'

15-16 In Greek mythology, Scylla and Charybdis were sea monsters that lived on either side of a narrow channel of water. When sailors tried to avoid one monster, they ended up sailing into the path of the other.

21 'enow' is short for 'enough'.

23-25 'it won't be long before we can't buy a single slice of bacon.' Christians can eat pork, but most Jews aren't allowed to — Lancelet is saying the price of pork will go up if too many Jews become Christians.

29 'keep cornering Jessica like this.'

36-37 'I can explain that better than you can explain getting a black-skinned woman pregnant'. Lorenzo thinks Lancelet should be ashamed of sleeping with someone who has black skin.

38 In the 16th century, 'Moor' was a word used to describe someone from North Africa.

39-41 'It's too bad that she's pregnant, but if she's less than an honourable woman, she's still more respectable than I thought.'

42-45 'Silence will soon be the best sign of intelligence, and talking will only be admired in parrots.'

Shakespeare's Techniques

Here, Lancelet makes a pun on the word "prepare" — he says that the servants are always prepared for dinner, as they've all got appetites. This creates humour.

48 'wit-snapper' means 'joker'.

50-52 'cover' means 'set the table', but also 'wear a hat'. Lorenzo uses the first meaning, but Lancelet replies as if he was using the second meaning.

Act Three

Act 3, Scene 5

63 'Good grief, he's got an answer to everything!'

Character — Lorenzo

Lorenzo is easily <u>frustrated</u> by Lancelet's <u>disobedience</u>. He isn't <u>quick-witted</u> enough to respond to Lancelet's <u>clever wordplay</u>.

67-68 'who use their way with words to hide what they mean.'

71 'More than I can say'.

71 'meet' means 'fitting'.

75 'merit' means 'deserve'.

77-80 'Imagine if two gods made a bet using women as their stakes — if one were to use Portia, the other would find it a hard bet to match'.

81-82 'I'm just as good a husband as Portia is a wife.'

83 'you should ask me to be the judge of that.'

Theme — Love

This scene isn't especially <u>romantic</u>, but it still shows the audience how <u>close</u> Lorenzo and Jessica are. Their conversation is <u>playful</u> and <u>flirtatious</u>.

LANCELET	For the table, sir, it shall be served in; for the meat, sir, it shall be covered; for your coming in to dinner, sir, why, let it be as humours and conceits shall govern.

60

Exit LANCELET

LORENZO	O dear discretion, how his words are suited! The fool hath planted in his memory An army of good words; and I do know A many fools, that stand in better place, Garnished like him, that for a tricksy word Defy the matter. How cheerest thou, Jessica? And now, good sweet, say thy opinion, How dost thou like the Lord Bassanio's wife?

65

70

JESSICA	Past all expressing. It is very meet The Lord Bassanio live an upright life; For, having such a blessing in his lady, He finds the joys of heaven here on earth; And if on earth he do not merit it, then In reason he should never come to heaven. Why, if two gods should play some heavenly match And on the wager lay two earthly women, And Portia one, there must be something else Pawned with the other, for the poor rude world Hath not her fellow.

75

80

LORENZO	Even such a husband Hast thou of me as she is for a wife.
JESSICA	Nay, but ask my opinion too of that.
LORENZO	I will anon: first, let us go to dinner.
JESSICA	Nay, let me praise you while I have a stomach.

85

LORENZO	No, pray thee, let it serve for table-talk; Then, howso'er thou speak'st, 'mong other things I shall digest it.
JESSICA	Well, I'll set you forth.

Exeunt

Character — Lancelet

Lancelet's <u>role</u> in the play is to <u>provide comedy</u>. The main way he does this is through <u>language</u> — he makes <u>rude jokes</u> and uses lots of <u>wordplay</u>. For example, in Act 3, Scene 5, he makes <u>puns</u> to deliberately <u>misinterpret</u> Lorenzo's instructions. Lancelet is funny to <u>watch</u> on stage, too. In Act 5, Scene 1, the <u>audience</u> is supposed to <u>enjoy</u> seeing him <u>struggle</u> to find Lorenzo <u>in the dark</u>.

Shakespeare also uses Lancelet to provide <u>comic relief</u>. Lancelet's appearance at the <u>end</u> of Act 3 is meant to <u>relieve</u> the <u>tension</u> in the audience so it can be <u>built up again</u> during Act 4, Scene 1.

Act Three — Practice Questions

Quick Questions

1) Which two characters mock Shylock in Act 3, Scene 1?

2) What does Shylock say he wouldn't have traded "for a wilderness of monkeys"?

3) In Act 3, Scene 2, what clue to the casket test is Bassanio given?

4) What does Portia give to Bassanio as a symbol of his commitment to her?

5) Apart from Bassanio and Portia, who else gets engaged in Act 3, Scene 2?

6) Who is the only person Antonio wants to see before he dies?

7) In Act 3, Scene 4, where does Portia tell Lorenzo she's going?

8) Why does Portia send a servant to Padua at the end of Act 3, Scene 4?

9) In Act 3, Scene 5, why does Lancelet think Jessica is "damned"?

In-depth Questions

1) Reread Act 3, Scene 1 (lines 24-71). Why does Shylock think it's fair for him to take revenge on Antonio?

2) What does Shylock's reaction to the news about Jessica reveal about his character?

3) Explain how the mood changes throughout Act 3, Scene 2.

4) Do you think Bassanio is more committed to Portia or Antonio? Explain your choice.

5) Why might denying Shylock his bond be harmful for Venice?

6) Explain how Shakespeare builds anticipation in Act 3, Scene 4.

7) Reread Act 3, Scene 5 (lines 30-41). How do you think a modern audience would react to this part of the play compared to an audience in Shakespeare's time?

8) Explain how Shakespeare uses puns to create humour in Act 3, Scene 5.

9) Imagine you're Bassanio. Write a reply to Antonio's letter from Act 3, Scene 2. Include your reaction to the bad news, as well as what you plan to do to help.

Act 4, Scene 1 — The Court Scene

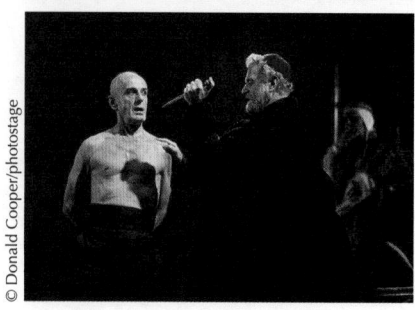

© Donald Cooper/photostage

Antonio goes on <u>trial</u>. Portia <u>intervenes</u> by <u>disguising</u> herself as a <u>lawyer</u>. She turns the <u>wording</u> of the bond against Shylock — she points out that he <u>can</u> take a pound of Antonio's <u>flesh</u>, but <u>not</u> a drop of his <u>blood</u>. The bond becomes <u>useless</u>. Shylock is <u>punished</u> for trying to <u>kill</u> Antonio, and Portia asks Bassanio for his <u>ring</u> as a <u>reward</u> for <u>saving</u> Antonio's <u>life</u>.

The '*Magnificoes*' are a group of the most important men in Venice.

Character — The Duke

The Duke is meant to be an <u>impartial judge</u>, but it's <u>clear</u> from the start of the scene that he's on <u>Antonio's side</u>.

3-4 'you're here to face a heartless enemy'.

6 A 'dram' is a very small amount of something.

6-8 'I've heard that you've gone out of your way to weaken his desire for revenge.'

8 'obdurate' means 'stubborn'.

Character — Antonio

Here, Antonio's "patience" and "quietness of spirit" are contrasted with Shylock's "rage". This makes the audience feel <u>sorry</u> for him.

17-21 In other words — 'Shylock, everyone thinks you're pretending that you want a pound of Antonio's flesh, and that you'll show mercy to him at the very last moment.'

24 In other words — 'spare his life'.

26 'part of his debt to you'.

29-31 'which would be enough to ruin even the wealthiest of merchants and earn sympathy from the hardest of hearts'.

32 In the 16th century, Tartars (who were a group of migrants from across central Asia) and Turks had a reputation for being cruel.

ACT 4, SCENE 1

VENICE. A COURT OF JUSTICE.

Enter the DUKE, *the* Magnificoes, ANTONIO, BASSANIO, GRATIANO, SALERIO *and others*

DUKE	What, is Antonio here?
ANTONIO	Ready, so please your grace.
DUKE	I am sorry for thee: thou art come to answer
	A stony adversary, an inhuman wretch
	uncapable of pity, void and empty 5
	From any dram of mercy.
ANTONIO	I have heard
	Your grace hath ta'en great pains to qualify
	His rigorous course; but since he stands obdurate
	And that no lawful means can carry me
	Out of his envy's reach, I do oppose 10
	My patience to his fury, and am armed
	To suffer, with a quietness of spirit,
	The very tyranny and rage of his.
DUKE	Go one, and call the Jew into the court.
SALERIO	He is ready at the door: he comes, my lord. 15

Enter SHYLOCK

DUKE	Make room, and let him stand before our face.
	Shylock, the world thinks, and I think so too,
	That thou but lead'st this fashion of thy malice
	To the last hour of act; and then 'tis thought
	Thou'lt show thy mercy and remorse more strange 20
	Than is thy strange apparent cruelty;
	And where thou now exact'st the penalty,
	Which is a pound of this poor merchant's flesh,
	Thou wilt not only loose the forfeiture,
	But, touched with human gentleness and love, 25
	Forgive a moiety of the principal;
	Glancing an eye of pity on his losses,
	That have of late so huddled on his back,
	Enow to press a royal merchant down
	And pluck commiseration of his state 30
	From brassy bosoms and rough hearts of flint,
	From stubborn Turks and Tartars, never trained
	To offices of tender courtesy.
	We all expect a gentle answer, Jew.

Act 4, Scene 1

SHYLOCK | I have possessed your grace of what I purpose; 35
And by our holy Sabbath have I sworn
To have the due and forfeit of my bond:
If you deny it, let the danger light
Upon your charter and your city's freedom.
You'll ask me, why I rather choose to have 40
A weight of carrion flesh than to receive
Three thousand ducats: I'll not answer that:
But, say, it is my humour: is it answered?
What if my house be troubled with a rat
And I be pleased to give ten thousand ducats 45
To have it baned? What, are you answered yet?
Some men there are love not a gaping pig;
Some, that are mad if they behold a cat;
And others, when the bagpipe sings i' the nose,
Cannot contain their urine: for affection, 50
Mistress of passion, sways it to the mood
Of what it likes or loathes. Now, for your answer:
As there is no firm reason to be rendered,
Why he cannot abide a gaping pig;
Why he, a harmless necessary cat; 55
Why he, a woollen bagpipe; but of force
Must yield to such inevitable shame
As to offend, himself being offended;
So can I give no reason, nor I will not,
More than a lodged hate and a certain loathing 60
I bear Antonio, that I follow thus
A losing suit against him. Are you answered?

BASSANIO | This is no answer, thou unfeeling man,
To excuse the current of thy cruelty.

SHYLOCK | I am not bound to please thee with my answers. 65

BASSANIO | Do all men kill the things they do not love?

SHYLOCK | Hates any man the thing he would not kill?

BASSANIO | Every offence is not a hate at first.

SHYLOCK | What, wouldst thou have a serpent sting thee
twice?

ANTONIO | I pray you, think you question with the Jew: 70
You may as well go stand upon the beach
And bid the main flood bate his usual height;
You may as well use question with the wolf
Why he hath made the ewe bleat for the lamb;
You may as well forbid the mountain pines 75
To wag their high tops and to make no noise,
When they are fretten with the gusts of heaven;
You may as well do anything most hard,
As seek to soften that — than which what's
harder? —
His Jewish heart: therefore, I do beseech you, 80
Make no more offers, use no farther means,
But with all brief and plain conveniency
Let me have judgment and the Jew his will.

---

35 'possessed' means 'informed'.

38-39 'If you deny me my bond, it will have dangerous consequences for trade in Venice' (see the top of p.50).

43 'Suppose I just feel like it — is that answer good enough for you?'

46 'baned' means 'poisoned'.

47 A 'gaping pig' is a pig cooked and served with its mouth open.

49-52 In other words — 'Others can't stand the nasal whine of bagpipes. We can't control what we love or hate'.

55 'necessary' means 'useful'.

56 'of force' means 'certainly'.

60 'lodged' means 'deep-rooted'.

62 In other words — 'A case I stand to gain nothing from'.

Shakespeare's Techniques

Short lines containing lots of monosyllabic words add to the hostile atmosphere by making the dialogue sound fast-paced and tense.

71-72 'You might as well stand on a beach telling the tide not to come in'.

Shakespeare's Techniques

Shakespeare uses natural imagery to emphasise how pointless it is to ask someone as evil as Shylock to be merciful.

77 'fretten' means 'disturbed'.

78-80 'There's no harder task than softening his Jewish heart'.

Act Four

Act 4, Scene 1

87 'draw' means 'accept'.

88 'rendering' means 'giving'.

92 'You use to carry out humiliating tasks'.

96-97 'let them eat the same food?'

Theme — Justice and Mercy

To Shylock, only the pound of Antonio's flesh will count as justice. The flesh is a symbol of his desire to see Antonio suffer for how he has treated him in the past.

101-102 'If you deny me my bond, then to hell with your laws! They are meaningless.'

105 'doctor' means 'lawyer'.

106 'determine' means 'settle'.

114-115 'I'm the sickly sheep of the flock, most suitable for death'.

118 An 'epitaph' is a short text written on someone's tombstone.

Shakespeare's Techniques

Shakespeare times Nerissa's entrance to make the scene more dramatic. She enters just when it seems certain that Antonio is doomed.

120 'whets' means 'sharpens'.

121 'earnestly' means 'eagerly'.

124-126 'No metal can be made half as keen as your desire for revenge, not even an executioner's axe.' Gratiano is making a pun on the word 'keen', which can mean 'sharp' or 'enthusiastic'.

BASSANIO	For thy three thousand ducats here is six.	
SHYLOCK	If every ducat in six thousand ducats	85
	Were in six parts and every part a ducat,	
	I would not draw them; I would have my bond.	
DUKE	How shalt thou hope for mercy, rendering none?	
SHYLOCK	What judgment shall I dread, doing no wrong?	
	You have among you many a purchased slave,	90
	Which, like your asses and your dogs and mules,	
	You use in abject and in slavish parts,	
	Because you bought them: shall I say to you,	
	Let them be free, marry them to your heirs?	
	Why sweat they under burdens? Let their beds	95
	Be made as soft as yours and let their palates	
	Be seasoned with such viands? You will answer	
	'The slaves are ours.' So do I answer you:	
	The pound of flesh, which I demand of him,	
	Is dearly bought; 'tis mine and I will have it.	100
	If you deny me, fie upon your law!	
	There is no force in the decrees of Venice.	
	I stand for judgment: answer; shall I have it?	
DUKE	Upon my power I may dismiss this court,	
	Unless Bellario, a learnèd doctor,	105
	Whom I have sent for to determine this,	
	Come here today.	
SALERIO	My lord, here stays without	
	A messenger with letters from the doctor,	
	New come from Padua.	
DUKE	Bring us the letter; call the messenger.	110
BASSANIO	Good cheer, Antonio! What, man, courage yet!	
	The Jew shall have my flesh, blood, bones and all,	
	Ere thou shalt lose for me one drop of blood.	
ANTONIO	I am a tainted wether of the flock,	
	Meetest for death: the weakest kind of fruit	115
	Drops earliest to the ground, and so let me;	
	You cannot better be employed, Bassanio,	
	Than to live still and write mine epitaph.	

Enter NERISSA, *dressed like a lawyer's clerk*

DUKE	Came you from Padua, from Bellario?	
NERISSA	From both. My lord Bellario greets your grace.	120
	(She presents a letter while Shylock whets his knife on his shoe)	
BASSANIO	Why dost thou whet thy knife so earnestly?	
SHYLOCK	To cut the forfeiture from that bankrupt there.	
GRATIANO	Not on thy sole, but on thy soul, harsh Jew,	
	Thou makest thy knife keen; but no metal can,	
	No, not the hangman's axe, bear half the keenness	125
	Of thy sharp envy. Can no prayers pierce thee?	
SHYLOCK	No, none that thou hast wit enough to make.	

Act 4, Scene 1

GRATIANO	O, be thou damned, inexecrable dog!
	And for thy life let justice be accused.
	Thou almost makest me waver in my faith	130
	To hold opinion with Pythagoras,
	That souls of animals infuse themselves
	Into the trunks of men: thy currish spirit
	Governed a wolf, who, hanged for human slaughter,
	Even from the gallows did his fell soul fleet,	135
	And, whilst thou lay'st in thy unhallowed dam,
	Infused itself in thee; for thy desires
	Are wolvish, bloody, starved and ravenous.
SHYLOCK	Till thou canst rail the seal from off my bond,
	Thou but offend'st thy lungs to speak so loud:	140
	Repair thy wit, good youth, or it will fall
	To cureless ruin. I stand here for law.
DUKE	This letter from Bellario doth commend
	A young and learnèd doctor to our court.
	Where is he?
NERISSA	He attendeth here hard by,	145
	To know your answer, whether you'll admit him.
DUKE	With all my heart. Some three or four of you
	Go give him courteous conduct to this place.

Exeunt some

	Meantime the court shall hear Bellario's letter.
	(Reads) "Your grace shall understand that at	150
	the receipt of your letter I am very sick: but in
	the instant that your messenger came, in loving
	visitation was with me a young doctor of Rome;
	his name is Balthasar. I acquainted him with
	the cause in controversy between the Jew and	155
	Antonio the merchant. We turned o'er many
	books together: he is furnished with my opinion;
	which — bettered with his own learning, the
	greatness whereof I cannot enough commend
	— comes with him, at my importunity, to fill up	160
	your grace's request in my stead. I beseech you,
	let his lack of years be no impediment to let him
	lack a reverend estimation; for I never knew so
	young a body with so old a head. I leave him to
	your gracious acceptance, whose trial shall better	165
	publish his commendation."
	You hear the learnèd Bellario, what he writes:
	And here, I take it, is the doctor come.

Enter PORTIA, dressed like a lawyer

	Give me your hand. Come you from old Bellario?
PORTIA	I did, my lord.
DUKE	You are welcome: take your place.	170

128 'inexecrable' means 'hateful'.

129 In other words — 'there's no justice in the fact that you're alive.'

131-137 Pythagoras was a Greek philosopher who believed that the souls of dead animals could enter human bodies. Gratiano is saying that the soul of a murderous wolf entered Shylock before he was born.

139-140 In other words — 'You're wasting your breath shouting at me, because it won't change anything'.

145 'hard by' means 'nearby'.

Character — Bellario

Although he never appears in person, Doctor Bellario has a significant role in this scene. His letter convinces the Duke to let Portia take part in the trial.

151-153 'but a young lawyer from Rome was paying me a friendly visit when your messenger arrived'.

155 'the argument in question'.

160 'at my importunity' means 'at my request'.

161-164 'I ask that you don't let his youth make you doubt his judgment, because I've never known someone so young show so much maturity'.

Shakespeare's Techniques

Unlike the men at the trial, the audience knows that the lawyer is actually Portia. This creates dramatic irony.

Act 4, Scene 1

171 'difference' means 'dispute'.

Character — Shylock

The answer to Portia's question would be obvious to an audience watching the play. Shylock's role as an outsider is often made clear by his costume.

179 'Can't stand in your way'.

180 'within his danger' means 'indebted to him'.

184-185 In other words — 'Mercy can't be forced. It comes naturally like rain falling from the heavens'.

Theme — Justice and Mercy

Portia's speech is powerful. She describes mercy using religious imagery, saying it's a blessing to those who give and receive it. This presents mercy as a Christian value.

188 'becomes' means 'suits'.

190 A 'sceptre' is a staff held by a monarch as a symbol of authority.

190 'temporal' means 'earthly'.

196-197 'Kings are most like God when they allow mercy to influence their sense of justice.'

199-200 'justice alone won't get any one of us into heaven'.

203 In other words — 'To get you to reconsider your claim'.

206 'I take full responsibility for my actions!' Shylock is saying that he's willing to accept the consequences of refusing to take pity on Antonio.

208 'discharge' means 'pay'.

209 'tender' means 'offer'.

215 'Use your authority to bend the rules just this once'.

Are you acquainted with the difference
That holds this present question in the court?

PORTIA I am informèd thoroughly of the cause.
Which is the merchant here, and which the Jew?

DUKE Antonio and old Shylock, both stand forth. 175

PORTIA Is your name Shylock?

SHYLOCK Shylock is my name.

PORTIA Of a strange nature is the suit you follow;
Yet in such rule that the Venetian law
Cannot impugn you as you do proceed.
You stand within his danger, do you not? 180

ANTONIO Ay, so he says.

PORTIA Do you confess the bond?

ANTONIO I do.

PORTIA Then must the Jew be merciful.

SHYLOCK On what compulsion must I? Tell me that.

PORTIA The quality of mercy is not strained,
It droppeth as the gentle rain from heaven 185
Upon the place beneath: it is twice blest;
It blesseth him that gives and him that takes:
'Tis mightiest in the mightiest: it becomes
The thronèd monarch better than his crown;
His sceptre shows the force of temporal power, 190
The attribute to awe and majesty,
Wherein doth sit the dread and fear of kings;
But mercy is above this sceptred sway;
It is enthronèd in the hearts of kings,
It is an attribute to God himself; 195
And earthly power doth then show likest God's
When mercy seasons justice. Therefore, Jew,
Though justice be thy plea, consider this,
That, in the course of justice, none of us
Should see salvation: we do pray for mercy; 200
And that same prayer doth teach us all to render
The deeds of mercy. I have spoke thus much
To mitigate the justice of thy plea;
Which if thou follow, this strict court of Venice
Must needs give sentence 'gainst the merchant
there. 205

SHYLOCK My deeds upon my head! I crave the law,
The penalty and forfeit of my bond.

PORTIA Is he not able to discharge the money?

BASSANIO Yes, here I tender it for him in the court;
Yea, twice the sum: if that will not suffice, 210
I will be bound to pay it ten times o'er,
On forfeit of my hands, my head, my heart:
If this will not suffice, it must appear
That malice bears down truth. And I beseech you,
Wrest once the law to your authority: 215

Act 4, Scene 1

	To do a great right, do a little wrong,	
	And curb this cruel devil of his will.	
PORTIA	It must not be; there is no power in Venice	
	Can alter a decree establishèd:	
	'Twill be recorded for a precedent,	220
	And many an error by the same example	
	Will rush into the state: it cannot be.	
SHYLOCK	A Daniel come to judgment! Yea, a Daniel!	
	O wise young judge, how I do honour thee!	
PORTIA	I pray you, let me look upon the bond.	225
SHYLOCK	Here 'tis, most reverend doctor, here it is.	
	(*Hands her the bond*)	
PORTIA	Shylock, there's thrice thy money offered thee.	
SHYLOCK	An oath, an oath, I have an oath in heaven:	
	Shall I lay perjury upon my soul?	
	No, not for Venice.	
PORTIA	Why, this bond is forfeit;	230
	And lawfully by this the Jew may claim	
	A pound of flesh, to be by him cut off	
	Nearest the merchant's heart. Be merciful:	
	Take thrice thy money; bid me tear the bond.	
SHYLOCK	When it is paid according to the tenor.	235
	It doth appear you are a worthy judge;	
	You know the law, your exposition	
	Hath been most sound: I charge you by the law,	
	Whereof you are a well-deserving pillar,	
	Proceed to judgment: by my soul I swear	240
	There is no power in the tongue of man	
	To alter me: I stay here on my bond.	
ANTONIO	Most heartily I do beseech the court	
	To give the judgment.	
PORTIA	Why then, thus it is:	
	You must prepare your bosom for his knife.	245
SHYLOCK	O noble judge! O excellent young man!	
PORTIA	For the intent and purpose of the law	
	Hath full relation to the penalty,	
	Which here appeareth due upon the bond.	
SHYLOCK	'Tis very true: O wise and upright judge!	250
	How much more elder art thou than thy looks!	
PORTIA	Therefore lay bare your bosom.	
SHYLOCK	Ay, his breast:	
	So says the bond: doth it not, noble judge?	
	'Nearest his heart', those are the very words.	
PORTIA	It is so. Are there balance here to weigh	255
	The flesh?	
SHYLOCK	I have them ready.	
PORTIA	Have by some surgeon, Shylock, on your charge,	
	To stop his wounds, lest he do bleed to death.	

Shakespeare's Techniques

When Portia admits that the rules can't be bent for Antonio, it creates tension. It makes it seem unlikely to the audience that she'll succeed in saving his life.

223 Daniel is a wise young man from the Bible. In one story, he saved a woman's life by intervening in her trial when she was falsely accused of a crime.

226 'reverend' means 'respected'.

229 'perjury' is when someone breaks an oath or makes a false promise. It's a sin in Judaism.

Character — Shylock

No amount of money can persuade Shylock to drop his case against Antonio. This shows how strong his desire for revenge is.

235 'tenor' means 'terms' (of the bond).

237 'exposition' means 'reasoning'.

241-242 'Nothing anyone says will change my mind — I want my bond.'

245 'bosom' means 'chest'.

247-249 In other words — 'The law fully supports the penalty set out in the bond.'

250 'upright' means 'honest'.

Character — Shylock

Shylock's exclamations make it seem like he's excited to kill Antonio. This makes it easier for the audience to see him as the villain of the play.

255 'balance' means 'scales'.

Act 4, Scene 1

SHYLOCK	Is it so nominated in the bond?	260
PORTIA	It is not so expressed: but what of that? 'Twere good you do so much for charity.	
SHYLOCK	*(Looking at the bond)* I cannot find it; 'tis not in the bond.	
PORTIA	You, merchant, have you anything to say?	
ANTONIO	But little: I am armed and well prepared. Give me your hand, Bassanio: fare you well! Grieve not that I am fallen to this for you; For herein Fortune shows herself more kind Than is her custom: it is still her use To let the wretched man outlive his wealth, To view with hollow eye and wrinkled brow An age of poverty; from which lingering penance Of such misery doth she cut me off. Commend me to your honourable wife: Tell her the process of Antonio's end; Say how I loved you, speak me fair in death; And, when the tale is told, bid her be judge Whether Bassanio had not once a love. Repent but you that you shall lose your friend, And he repents not that he pays your debt; For if the Jew do cut but deep enough, I'll pay it presently with all my heart.	265 270 275 280
BASSANIO	Antonio, I am married to a wife Which is as dear to me as life itself; But life itself, my wife, and all the world, Are not with me esteemed above thy life: I would lose all, ay, sacrifice them all Here to this devil, to deliver you.	285
PORTIA	Your wife would give you little thanks for that, If she were by, to hear you make the offer.	290
GRATIANO	I have a wife, whom, I protest, I love: I would she were in heaven, so she could Entreat some power to change this currish Jew.	
NERISSA	'Tis well you offer it behind her back; The wish would make else an unquiet house.	295
SHYLOCK	These be the Christian husbands. I have a daughter; Would any of the stock of Barabbas Had been her husband rather than a Christian! We trifle time: I pray thee, pursue sentence.	
PORTIA	A pound of that same merchant's flesh is thine: The court awards it, and the law doth give it.	300
SHYLOCK	Most rightful judge!	
PORTIA	And you must cut this flesh from off his breast: The law allows it, and the court awards it.	
SHYLOCK	Most learnèd judge! A sentence! Come, prepare!	305
PORTIA	Tarry a little; there is something else.	

Side notes:

262 'out of kindness'.

265 'Not much — I'm ready to accept my fate.'

268 Fortune (or Fortuna) was the Roman goddess of luck and fate.

269-273 In other words — 'She (Fortune) usually lets men outlive their wealth and forces them to spend their old age in poverty, but I won't have to endure that misery.'

278 'love' means 'loving friend'.

Theme — Love
Antonio and Bassanio are willing to make huge sacrifices for each other. This shows how important their friendship is to them.

286 'esteemed' means 'valued'.

Shakespeare's Techniques
Bassanio and Gratiano don't realise that their wives have heard what they've said. Their failure to recognise Portia and Nerissa is the main source of humour in this scene.

296 'That's what you get for marrying a Christian.'

297 'the descendants of Barabbas'. In the Bible, Barabbas was a Jewish criminal who was released instead of Jesus not long before Jesus was killed.

299 'trifle' means 'waste'.

306 'Wait a moment'.

Act 4, Scene 1

This bond doth give thee here no jot of blood;
The words expressly are 'a pound of flesh'.
Take then thy bond, take thou thy pound of flesh;
But, in the cutting it, if thou dost shed   310
One drop of Christian blood, thy lands and goods
Are, by the laws of Venice, confiscate
Unto the state of Venice.

GRATIANO   O upright judge! Mark, Jew: O learnèd judge!

SHYLOCK   Is that the law?

PORTIA   Thyself shalt see the act: 315
For, as thou urgest justice, be assured
Thou shalt have justice, more than thou desirest.

GRATIANO   O learnèd judge! Mark, Jew: a learnèd judge!

SHYLOCK   I take this offer, then; pay the bond thrice
And let the Christian go.

BASSANIO   Here is the money.   320

PORTIA   Soft!
The Jew shall have all justice. Soft, no haste:
He shall have nothing but the penalty.

GRATIANO   O Jew! An upright judge, a learnèd judge!

PORTIA   Therefore prepare thee to cut off the flesh.   325
Shed thou no blood, nor cut thou less nor more
But just a pound of flesh: if thou cut'st more
Or less than a just pound, be it but so much
As makes it light or heavy in the substance,
Or the division of the twentieth part   330
Of one poor scruple, nay, if the scale do turn
But in the estimation of a hair,
Thou diest and all thy goods are confiscate.

GRATIANO   A second Daniel, a Daniel, Jew!
Now, infidel, I have thee on the hip.   335

PORTIA   Why doth the Jew pause? Take thy forfeiture.

SHYLOCK   Give me my principal, and let me go.

BASSANIO   I have it ready for thee; here it is.

PORTIA   He hath refused it in the open court:
He shall have merely justice and his bond.   340

GRATIANO   A Daniel, still say I, a second Daniel!
I thank thee, Jew, for teaching me that word.

SHYLOCK   Shall I not have barely my principal?

PORTIA   Thou shalt have nothing but the forfeiture,
To be so taken at thy peril, Jew.   345

SHYLOCK   Why, then the devil give him good of it!
I'll stay no longer question. (Begins to go)

PORTIA   Tarry, Jew:
The law hath yet another hold on you.
It is enacted in the laws of Venice,
If it be proved against an alien   350
That by direct or indirect attempts

Theme — Justice and Mercy

Shylock insists on receiving the exact terms of his bond, but Portia cleverly turns this against him. The bond says Shylock can take a pound of Antonio's flesh, but it doesn't mention any blood.

308 'expressly' means 'exactly'.

311-313 'according to Venetian law, your lands and property will be seized by the state of Venice.'

315 'You'll soon see for yourself.'

Character — Gratiano

Gratiano imitates Shylock's praise of Portia from earlier in the scene to mock him. This would make him seem cruel to a modern audience.

321 'Soft!' means 'Not so fast!'

328-333 In other words — 'If it's lighter or heavier by a fraction of an ounce, or if it tips the scales by a hair's breadth, you'll die and everything you own will be seized.'

335 'I've got you at a disadvantage.'

337 The 'principal' is the amount of money Antonio borrowed from Shylock (three thousand ducats).

Theme — Justice and Mercy

Shylock's stubbornness causes his downfall. Earlier in the scene, he refused to take the money and show Antonio mercy, so Portia isn't prepared to let him backtrack and take it now.

346-347 'I'll let the devil deal with him, then! I've finished arguing this case.'

349 'enacted' means 'stated'.

350 'alien' means 'foreigner'.

Act 4, Scene 1

353-355 'Half of all he owns will go to the person he tried to kill — the other half will go to the state.'

357 'no matter what anyone else says'.

362-363 'you've earned the punishment I just described.'

Character — The Duke

The Duke decides to spare Shylock's life. This makes him seem honourable, as he encouraged Shylock to spare Antonio's life earlier in the scene.

373 'Which might be reduced to a fine if you (Shylock) show remorse.'

Theme — Reality and Appearance

Shylock claims that these punishments have made his life no longer worth living. This causes the audience to question if the law is really as fair as it appears.

380 'Give him a noose for free'.

385-386 In other words — 'Lorenzo'.

Theme — Justice and Mercy

Antonio might think he's being merciful here — 16th-century Christians believed all Jews went to hell, so Antonio could be trying to save Shylock's soul.

388 'presently' means 'now'.

392 'recant' means 'take back'.

395 A 'deed of gift' is an official document that transfers money or any other kind of property from one person to another.

	He seek the life of any citizen,	
	The party 'gainst the which he doth contrive	
	Shall seize one half his goods; the other half	
	Comes to the privy coffer of the state;	355
	And the offender's life lies in the mercy	
	Of the duke only, 'gainst all other voice.	
	In which predicament, I say, thou stand'st;	
	For it appears, by manifest proceeding,	
	That indirectly and directly too	360
	Thou hast contrived against the very life	
	Of the defendant; and thou hast incurred	
	The danger formerly by me rehearsed.	
	Down therefore and beg mercy of the duke.	
GRATIANO	Beg that thou mayst have leave to hang thyself:	365
	And yet, thy wealth being forfeit to the state,	
	Thou hast not left the value of a cord;	
	Therefore thou must be hanged at the state's charge.	
DUKE	That thou shalt see the difference of our spirits,	
	I pardon thee thy life before thou ask it:	370
	For half thy wealth, it is Antonio's;	
	The other half comes to the general state,	
	Which humbleness may drive unto a fine.	
PORTIA	Ay, for the state, not for Antonio.	
SHYLOCK	Nay, take my life and all; pardon not that:	375
	You take my house when you do take the prop	
	That doth sustain my house; you take my life	
	When you do take the means whereby I live.	
PORTIA	What mercy can you render him, Antonio?	
GRATIANO	A halter gratis; nothing else, for God's sake.	380
ANTONIO	So please my lord the duke and all the court	
	To quit the fine for one half of his goods,	
	I am content; so he will let me have	
	The other half in use, to render it,	
	Upon his death, unto the gentleman	385
	That lately stole his daughter:	
	Two things provided more, that, for this favour,	
	He presently become a Christian;	
	The other, that he do record a gift,	
	Here in the court, of all he dies possessed,	390
	Unto his son Lorenzo and his daughter.	
DUKE	He shall do this, or else I do recant	
	The pardon that I late pronouncèd here.	
PORTIA	Art thou contented, Jew? What dost thou say?	
SHYLOCK	I am content.	
PORTIA	Clerk, draw a deed of gift.	395
SHYLOCK	I pray you, give me leave to go from hence;	
	I am not well: send the deed after me,	
	And I will sign it.	
DUKE	Get thee gone, but do it.	

Act 4, Scene 1

GRATIANO	In christening shalt thou have two godfathers:
	Had I been judge, thou shouldst have had ten more, 400
	To bring thee to the gallows, not the font.

Exit SHYLOCK

DUKE	Sir, I entreat you home with me to dinner.
PORTIA	I humbly do desire your grace of pardon:
	I must away this night toward Padua,
	And it is meet I presently set forth. 405
DUKE	I am sorry that your leisure serves you not.
	Antonio, gratify this gentleman,
	For, in my mind, you are much bound to him.

Exeunt DUKE *and his train*

BASSANIO	Most worthy gentleman, I and my friend
	Have by your wisdom been this day acquitted 410
	Of grievous penalties; in lieu whereof,
	Three thousand ducats, due unto the Jew,
	We freely cope your courteous pains withal.
ANTONIO	And stand indebted, over and above,
	In love and service to you evermore. 415
PORTIA	He is well paid that is well satisfied;
	And I, delivering you, am satisfied
	And therein do account myself well paid:
	My mind was never yet more mercenary.
	I pray you, know me when we meet again: 420
	I wish you well, and so I take my leave.
	(Starts to leave)
BASSANIO	Dear sir, of force I must attempt you further:
	Take some remembrance of us, as a tribute,
	Not as a fee: grant me two things, I pray you,
	Not to deny me, and to pardon me. 425
PORTIA	You press me far, and therefore I will yield.
	(To Antonio) Give me your gloves, I'll wear them for your sake;
	(To Bassanio) And, for your love, I'll take this ring from you:
	Do not draw back your hand; I'll take no more;
	And you in love shall not deny me this. 430
BASSANIO	This ring, good sir, alas, it is a trifle!
	I will not shame myself to give you this.
PORTIA	I will have nothing else but only this;
	And now methinks I have a mind to it.
BASSANIO	There's more depends on this than on the value. 435
	The dearest ring in Venice will I give you,
	And find it out by proclamation:
	Only for this, I pray you, pardon me.
PORTIA	I see, sir, you are liberal in offers.
	You taught me first to beg; and now methinks 440
	You teach me how a beggar should be answered.

399-401 'You'll get two godfathers at your christening. If I'd been your judge, you would have had twelve (i.e. a jury) to hang you instead.'

Shakespeare's Techniques

This is the last time Shylock appears on stage. His exit signals a shift towards a lighter mood that lasts from here to the end of the play.

405 'And I need to leave at once.'

407 'gratify' means 'reward'.

410 'acquitted' means 'cleared'.

Shakespeare's Techniques

Bassanio doesn't know he's talking to Portia. It's funny to see him offer her money that belonged to her in the first place as a reward.

417 'delivering' means 'saving'.

419 'I didn't do it for the money.'

422 'I'm afraid I have to insist'.

Character — Portia

Portia is testing Bassanio's loyalty here. This shows that she's strong-minded.

431 'a trifle' means 'nothing'. Bassanio is down-playing the value of the ring to convince Portia that she doesn't want it.

435 'This isn't just valuable to me for financial reasons.'

437 'by proclamation' means 'with a public advertisement'.

439 In other words — 'I see you aren't as generous as you seemed.'

Act 4, Scene 2 — Nerissa Joins the Fun

Bassanio initially resists when Portia asks for his ring. He is loyal to her — just not as loyal as Portia would like.

445 'Many men use the same excuse to avoid giving gifts away.'

448 'hold it against you'.

Theme — Love

Bassanio's loyalties are torn. He's been forced to choose between his love for his wife and his best friend.

456 'thither' means 'go there'.

BASSANIO	Good sir, this ring was given me by my wife;
	And when she put it on, she made me vow
	That I should neither sell nor give nor lose it.
PORTIA	That 'scuse serves many men to save their gifts. 445
	An if your wife be not a madwoman,
	And know how well I have deserved the ring,
	She would not hold out enemy for ever,
	For giving it to me. Well, peace be with you!

Exeunt PORTIA *and* NERISSA

ANTONIO	My lord Bassanio, let him have the ring: 450
	Let his deservings and my love withal
	Be valued against your wife's commandment.
BASSANIO	Go, Gratiano, run and overtake him;
	Give him the ring, and bring him, if thou canst,
	Unto Antonio's house: away! Make haste. 455

Exit GRATIANO

	Come, you and I will thither presently;
	And in the morning early will we both
	Fly toward Belmont: come, Antonio.

Exeunt

Gratiano catches up with Portia in the street and gives her Bassanio's ring. Nerissa decides to see if she can get Gratiano to give his ring away as well.

ACT 4, SCENE 2

1 'Find out where the Jew lives'.

5 'I'm glad I've caught you.'

7 'entreat' means 'request'.

11 'my young assistant' (Nerissa).

VENICE. A STREET.

Enter PORTIA *and* NERISSA, *still disguised*

PORTIA	Inquire the Jew's house out, give him this deed
	And let him sign it: we'll away tonight
	And be a day before our husbands home:
	This deed will be well welcome to Lorenzo.

Enter GRATIANO

GRATIANO	Fair sir, you are well o'erta'en. 5
	My lord Bassanio upon more advice
	Hath sent you here this ring, and doth entreat
	Your company at dinner.
PORTIA	That cannot be:
	His ring I do accept most thankfully:
	And so, I pray you, tell him: furthermore, 10
	I pray you, show my youth old Shylock's house.

Act Four

Practice Questions

GRATIANO	That will I do.
NERISSA	Sir, I would speak with you.
	(*Aside to Portia*) I'll see if I can get my husband's ring,
	Which I did make him swear to keep for ever.
PORTIA	(*Aside to Nerissa*) Thou mayst, I warrant.
	We shall have old swearing 15
	That they did give the rings away to men;
	But we'll outface them, and outswear them too.
	(*Aloud*) Away! Make haste: thou know'st where I will tarry.
NERISSA	Come, good sir, will you show me to this house?
	Exeunt

Character — Nerissa

Nerissa's decision to test Gratiano's <u>loyalty</u> shows that she is <u>strong-willed</u> and <u>spirited</u>, like <u>Portia</u>.

15-17 In other words — 'I bet you can do it. They'll swear they gave the rings to men, but we'll confront them and get the better of them.'

Quick Questions

1) Reread Act 4, Scene 1 (lines 35-62). What reason does Shylock give for wanting to take a pound of Antonio's flesh?

2) Why does Shylock refer to Portia as "a Daniel"?

3) How does Portia stop Shylock from taking a pound of Antonio's flesh?

4) What action makes the Duke stand out as an honourable character?

5) What three punishments does Shylock receive for trying to kill Antonio?

6) What are Portia and Nerissa testing when they ask their husbands for their rings?

In-depth Questions

1) In Act 4, Scene 1, how does Shakespeare make the audience feel sympathy for Antonio?

2) Compare Portia and Shylock's attitudes to mercy in Act 4, Scene 1.

3) Explain how Shakespeare creates a tense atmosphere in Act 4, Scene 1.

4) Why do you think Antonio forces Shylock to become a Christian?

5) Do you think the outcome of Antonio's trial is fair? Explain why / why not.

6) Reread Act 4, Scene 2. Rewrite this scene in modern English.

Act 5, Scene 1 — Everyone Gathers in Belmont

© Donald Cooper/photostage

Portia and Nerissa <u>return</u> to <u>Belmont</u>, followed soon after by their <u>husbands</u> and <u>Antonio</u>. Bassanio and Gratiano are <u>criticised</u> by their wives for giving their <u>rings</u> away, but Portia eventually <u>reveals</u> that she was the <u>lawyer</u> and Nerissa was her <u>assistant</u> all along. All of the couples are <u>happily reconciled</u>.

Shakespeare's Techniques

The references in lines 1-14 are from <u>classical mythology</u>. The stories aren't <u>well-known</u> today, but they'd probably have been <u>recognised</u> by Shakespeare's audience.

4-6 Troilus and Cressida were lovers who were separated by a great war. Cressida swore to remain faithful, but gave her love to someone else.

7-9 Thisbe went to meet her lover, Pyramus, but ran away from their meeting place when she saw a lion. When Pyramus arrived, he assumed Thisbe was dead and killed himself.

10-12 Dido was Queen of Carthage. She committed suicide after finding out her lover, Aeneas, had set sail from Carthage and abandoned her.

13-14 Medea healed her husband's father, Aeson, but was abandoned by her husband some years later.

16 'with her big-spending lover'.

Theme — Love

The start of this scene shows how <u>close</u> Lorenzo and Jessica are to each other. Their <u>shared lines</u> of <u>blank verse</u> suggest that they <u>belong together</u>.

21 A 'shrew' is an ill-tempered woman.

23 'I'd outdo you at talking about the night if nobody was coming'.

24 'footing' means 'footsteps'.

ACT 5, SCENE 1

BELMONT. AVENUE TO PORTIA'S HOUSE.

Enter LORENZO *and* JESSICA

LORENZO	The moon shines bright: in such a night as this,	
	When the sweet wind did gently kiss the trees	
	And they did make no noise, in such a night	
	Troilus methinks mounted the Trojan walls	
	And sighed his soul toward the Grecian tents,	5
	Where Cressid lay that night.	
JESSICA	In such a night	
	Did Thisbe fearfully o'ertrip the dew	
	And saw the lion's shadow ere himself	
	And ran dismayed away.	
LORENZO	In such a night	
	Stood Dido with a willow in her hand	10
	Upon the wild sea banks and waft her love	
	To come again to Carthage.	
JESSICA	In such a night	
	Medea gathered the enchanted herbs	
	That did renew old Aeson.	
LORENZO	In such a night	
	Did Jessica steal from the wealthy Jew	15
	And with an unthrift love did run from Venice	
	As far as Belmont.	
JESSICA	In such a night	
	Did young Lorenzo swear he loved her well,	
	Stealing her soul with many vows of faith	
	And ne'er a true one.	
LORENZO	In such a night	20
	Did pretty Jessica, like a little shrew,	
	Slander her love, and he forgave it her.	
JESSICA	I would out-night you, did nobody come;	
	But hark, I hear the footing of a man.	

Enter STEPHANO

LORENZO	Who comes so fast in silence of the night?	25
STEPHANO	A friend.	
LORENZO	A friend! What friend? Your name, I pray you, friend?	

Act 5, Scene 1

STEPHANO	Stephano is my name; and I bring word
	My mistress will before the break of day
	Be here at Belmont; she doth stray about 30
	By holy crosses, where she kneels and prays
	For happy wedlock hours.
LORENZO	Who comes with her?
STEPHANO	None but a holy hermit and her maid.
	I pray you, is my master yet returned?
LORENZO	He is not, nor we have not heard from him. 35
	But go we in, I pray thee, Jessica,
	And ceremoniously let us prepare
	Some welcome for the mistress of the house.

Enter LANCELET

LANCELET	Sola, sola! Wo ha, ho! Sola, sola!
LORENZO	Who calls? 40
LANCELET	Sola! Did you see Master Lorenzo?
	Master Lorenzo, sola, sola!
LORENZO	Leave hollowing, man! Here.
LANCELET	Sola! Where, where?
LORENZO	Here. 45
LANCELET	Tell him there's a post come from my master, with
	his horn full of good news: my master will be here
	ere morning.

Exit LANCELET

LORENZO	Sweet soul, let's in, and there expect their coming.
	And yet no matter: why should we go in? 50
	My friend Stephano, signify, I pray you,
	Within the house, your mistress is at hand;
	And bring your music forth into the air.

Exit STEPHANO

How sweet the moonlight sleeps upon this bank!
Here will we sit and let the sounds of music   55
Creep in our ears: soft stillness and the night
Become the touches of sweet harmony.
Sit, Jessica. Look how the floor of heaven
Is thick inlaid with patines of bright gold:
There's not the smallest orb which thou behold'st   60
But in his motion like an angel sings,
Still quiring to the young-eyed cherubins;
Such harmony is in immortal souls;
But whilst this muddy vesture of decay
Doth grossly close it in, we cannot hear it.   65

Enter Musicians

Come, ho! And wake Diana with a hymn!
With sweetest touches pierce your mistress' ear,
And draw her home with music.

Music plays

30-32 'she's been delayed by the shrines along the road, where she stops to pray for a happy marriage.'

39 These exclamations are calls used to get the attention of animals.

Character — Lancelet

Lancelet provides humour again here (see p.54). It's funny to watch him trying to find Lorenzo in the dark.

43 'Stop shouting, man!'

46 'post' means 'messenger'.

48 'ere' means 'before'.

51-52 'let the servants know that their mistress is coming'.

Shakespeare's Techniques

The way that Lorenzo uses natural imagery to describe his surroundings gives the audience a sense of what a peaceful setting Belmont is.

58-62 In other words — 'Look at how the sky is studded with bright gold stars. Not one of them moves without singing in harmony with the others, like an angelic choir'.

63-65 'The same harmony exists in our souls, but we can't hear it when it's trapped in our mortal bodies'.

66 Diana was the Roman goddess of nature and the moon.

Shakespeare's Techniques

Shakespeare uses music to create a romantic mood in this part of the scene.

Act Five

Act 5, Scene 1

70 'That's because your soul is in tune with the music'.

71 'wanton' means 'unrestrained'.

72 'colts' are young male horses.

75 'perchance' means 'perhaps'.

77 'come to a halt'.

79-80 The 'poet' referred to is Ovid. Ovid wrote a poem about Orpheus, a legendary musician who charmed trees, rocks and rivers with his music.

81 'stockish' means 'unfeeling'.

Character — Shylock

These lines might refer to Shylock, who tells Jessica to shut music out of his house in Act 2, Scene 5. This reinforces his image as an unpleasant character.

87 In Greek mythology, Erebus was a place of darkness that the dead had to pass through in order to reach the underworld.

Shakespeare's Techniques

This scene contains a lot of references to the night. Scenery was very basic in Shakespeare's time, so he's relying on language to communicate the setting.

94-97 'A deputy seems as powerful as a king until the king is present — after that, the deputy's power drains away like a river drains into the sea.'

99 In other words — 'Things can only be good if they take place under the right circumstances'.

103 'attended' means 'heard'.

109 In Greek mythology, Endymion was so handsome that the goddess of the moon fell in love with him as he slept. His sleep was made to last forever so she could always visit him.

JESSICA	I am never merry when I hear sweet music.	
LORENZO	The reason is, your spirits are attentive:	70
	For do but note a wild and wanton herd,	
	Or race of youthful and unhandled colts,	
	Fetching mad bounds, bellowing and neighing loud,	
	Which is the hot condition of their blood;	
	If they but hear perchance a trumpet sound,	75
	Or any air of music touch their ears,	
	You shall perceive them make a mutual stand,	
	Their savage eyes turned to a modest gaze	
	By the sweet power of music: therefore the poet	
	Did feign that Orpheus drew trees, stones and floods;	80
	Since nought so stockish, hard and full of rage,	
	But music for the time doth change his nature.	
	The man that hath no music in himself,	
	Nor is not moved with concord of sweet sounds,	
	Is fit for treasons, stratagems and spoils;	85
	The motions of his spirit are dull as night	
	And his affections dark as Erebus:	
	Let no such man be trusted. Mark the music.	

Enter PORTIA *and* NERISSA

PORTIA	That light we see is burning in my hall.	
	How far that little candle throws his beams!	90
	So shines a good deed in a naughty world.	
NERISSA	When the moon shone, we did not see the candle.	
PORTIA	So doth the greater glory dim the less:	
	A substitute shines brightly as a king	
	Until the king be by, and then his state	95
	Empties itself, as doth an inland brook	
	Into the main of waters. Music! Hark!	

Music plays

NERISSA	It is your music, madam, of the house.	
PORTIA	Nothing is good, I see, without respect:	
	Methinks it sounds much sweeter than by day.	100
NERISSA	Silence bestows that virtue on it, madam.	
PORTIA	The crow doth sing as sweetly as the lark,	
	When neither is attended, and I think	
	The nightingale, if she should sing by day,	
	When every goose is cackling, would be thought	105
	No better a musician than the wren.	
	How many things by season seasoned are	
	To their right praise and true perfection!	
	Peace, ho! The moon sleeps with Endymion	
	And would not be awaked.	

Music ceases

LORENZO	That is the voice,	110
	Or I am much deceived, of Portia.	

Act 5, Scene 1

PORTIA	He knows me as the blind man knows the cuckoo, By the bad voice.
LORENZO	Dear lady, welcome home.
PORTIA	We have been praying for our husbands' healths, Which speed, we hope, the better for our words. Are they returned?	115
LORENZO	Madam, they are not yet; But there is come a messenger before, To signify their coming.
PORTIA	Go in, Nerissa; Give order to my servants that they take No note at all of our being absent hence; Nor you, Lorenzo; Jessica, nor you.	120

A tucket *sounds*

| LORENZO | Your husband is at hand; I hear his trumpet: We are no tell-tales, madam; fear you not. |
| PORTIA | This night methinks is but the daylight sick; It looks a little paler: 'tis a day, Such as the day is when the sun is hid. | 125 |

Enter BASSANIO, ANTONIO, GRATIANO *and their followers*

BASSANIO	We should hold day with the Antipodes, If you would walk in absence of the sun.
PORTIA	Let me give light, but let me not be light; For a light wife doth make a heavy husband, And never be Bassanio so for me: But God sort all! You are welcome home, my lord.	130
BASSANIO	I thank you, madam. Give welcome to my friend. This is the man, this is Antonio, To whom I am so infinitely bound.	135
PORTIA	You should in all sense be much bound to him. For, as I hear, he was much bound for you.
ANTONIO	No more than I am well acquitted of.
PORTIA	Sir, you are very welcome to our house: It must appear in other ways than words, Therefore I scant this breathing courtesy.	140
GRATIANO	(*To Nerissa*) By yonder moon I swear you do me wrong; In faith, I gave it to the judge's clerk: Would he were gelt that had it, for my part, Since you do take it, love, so much at heart.	145
PORTIA	A quarrel, ho, already? What's the matter?
GRATIANO	About a hoop of gold, a paltry ring That she did give me, whose posy was For all the world like cutler's poetry Upon a knife, 'Love me, and leave me not.'	150
NERISSA	What talk you of the posy or the value? You swore to me, when I did give it you,

Theme — Reality and Appearance

Portia's lie is so convincing because it's exactly what Lorenzo would expect to hear — 16th-century women weren't involved in public affairs, so Portia is expected to wait patiently for Bassanio to come back.

121 A 'tucket' is a short tune played on a horn or trumpet.

Theme — Love

Bassanio sounds like a courtly lover here — he uses the poetic language knights used to impress their lovers in medieval literature. This makes him seem romantic.

127 'the other side of the world'.

129-130 'An unfaithful wife creates an unhappy husband, and I wouldn't want to make Bassanio unhappy'.

136-137 'You should feel bound to him in every way, as he got into a bind (i.e. a tricky situation) for you.'

141 'scant' means 'cut short'.

141 'breathing' means 'spoken'.

144-145 'I wish the clerk I gave it to had been castrated (had his testicles removed), since you've got so upset.'

147 'paltry' means 'worthless'.

148 A 'posy' is an inscription engraved on the inside of a ring.

149-150 'no better than the poetry a knife-maker engraves on a knife'.

Act Five

Act 5, Scene 1

155 'vehement' means 'forceful'.

158 'The lawyer's assistant you gave it to will never grow a beard.' Nerissa is implying that Gratiano gave the ring to another woman.

162 'scrubbèd' means 'undersized'.

164 'prating' means 'babbling'.

167 'slightly' means 'easily'.

Shakespeare's Techniques

When Portia pretends not to realise that Bassanio has given away his ring, it creates dramatic irony — the audience knows that she's the one who took it.

173-174 'for all the money in the world'.

182 'Who went to a lot of trouble doing all that writing (at the trial)'.

Character — Gratiano

Gratiano's excuse for giving away his ring isn't as strong as Bassanio's. This suggests that he isn't as committed to his wife as Bassanio is.

186-187 'If I could make it better by lying, I would'.

199 'abate' means 'lessen'.

Theme — Love

Portia thinks Bassanio doesn't fully appreciate the importance of their marriage. This is why she tricks him — she wants him to put their love before his friendship with Antonio.

	That you would wear it till your hour of death
	And that it should lie with you in your grave:
	Though not for me, yet for your vehement oaths,
	You should have been respective and have kept it.
	Gave it a judge's clerk! No, God's my judge,
	The clerk will ne'er wear hair on's face that had it.
GRATIANO	He will, an if he live to be a man.
NERISSA	Ay, if a woman live to be a man.
GRATIANO	Now, by this hand, I gave it to a youth,
	A kind of boy, a little scrubbèd boy,
	No higher than thyself; the judge's clerk,
	A prating boy, that begged it as a fee:
	I could not for my heart deny it him.
PORTIA	You were to blame, I must be plain with you,
	To part so slightly with your wife's first gift:
	A thing stuck on with oaths upon your finger
	And so riveted with faith unto your flesh.
	I gave my love a ring and made him swear
	Never to part with it; and here he stands;
	I dare be sworn for him he would not leave it
	Nor pluck it from his finger, for the wealth
	That the world masters. Now, in faith, Gratiano,
	You give your wife too unkind a cause of grief:
	An 'twere to me, I should be mad at it.
BASSANIO	*(Aside)* Why, I were best to cut my left hand off
	And swear I lost the ring defending it.
GRATIANO	My Lord Bassanio gave his ring away
	Unto the judge that begged it and indeed
	Deserved it too; and then the boy, his clerk,
	That took some pains in writing, he begged mine;
	And neither man nor master would take aught
	But the two rings.
PORTIA	What ring gave you my lord?
	Not that, I hope, which you received of me.
BASSANIO	If I could add a lie unto a fault,
	I would deny it; but you see my finger
	Hath not the ring upon it; it is gone.
PORTIA	Even so void is your false heart of truth.
	By heaven, I will ne'er come in your bed
	Until I see the ring.
NERISSA	Nor I in yours till I again see mine.
BASSANIO	Sweet Portia,
	If you did know to whom I gave the ring,
	If you did know for whom I gave the ring
	And would conceive for what I gave the ring
	And how unwillingly I left the ring,
	When nought would be accepted but the ring,
	You would abate the strength of your displeasure.
PORTIA	If you had known the virtue of the ring,
	Or half her worthiness that gave the ring,

155

160

165

170

175

180

185

190

195

200

Act 5, Scene 1

Or your own honour to contain the ring,
You would not then have parted with the ring.
What man is there so much unreasonable,
If you had pleased to have defended it   205
With any terms of zeal, wanted the modesty
To urge the thing held as a ceremony?
Nerissa teaches me what to believe:
I'll die for't but some woman had the ring.

BASSANIO   No, by mine honour, madam, by my soul,   210
No woman had it, but a civil doctor,
Which did refuse three thousand ducats of me
And begged the ring; the which I did deny him
And suffered him to go displeased away;
Even he that did uphold the very life   215
Of my dear friend. What should I say, sweet lady?
I was enforced to send it after him;
I was beset with shame and courtesy;
My honour would not let ingratitude
So much besmear it. Pardon me, good lady;   220
For, by these blessèd candles of the night,
Had you been there, I think you would have begged
The ring of me to give the worthy doctor.

PORTIA   Let not that doctor e'er come near my house:
Since he hath got the jewel that I loved,   225
And that which you did swear to keep for me,
I will become as liberal as you;
I'll not deny him anything I have,
No, not my body nor my husband's bed:
Know him I shall, I am well sure of it: 230
Lie not a night from home; watch me like Argus:
If you do not, if I be left alone,
Now, by mine honour, which is yet mine own,
I'll have that doctor for my bedfellow.

NERISSA   And I his clerk; therefore be well advised   235
How you do leave me to mine own protection.

GRATIANO   Well, do you so; let not me take him, then;
For if I do, I'll mar the young clerk's pen.

ANTONIO   I am the unhappy subject of these quarrels.

PORTIA   Sir, grieve not you; you are welcome
                                   notwithstanding.   240

BASSANIO   Portia, forgive me this enforcèd wrong;
And, in the hearing of these many friends,
I swear to thee, even by thine own fair eyes,
Wherein I see myself —

PORTIA   Mark you but that!
In both my eyes he doubly sees himself;   245
In each eye, one: swear by your double self,
And there's an oath of credit.

BASSANIO   Nay, but hear me:
Pardon this fault, and by my soul I swear

204-207 'What man would be so unreasonable to demand your ring from you if you had argued to keep it with any real enthusiasm?'

209 'I'd bet my life that you gave the ring to some woman.'

211 'doctor' means 'lawyer'.

Character — Bassanio

Bassanio's account is true. He didn't want to give his ring to Portia, and only gave in when he felt like he had no other choice.

218 'beset' means 'overcome'.

219-220 'My sense of honour wouldn't let me be so ungrateful.'

221 'blessèd candles of the night' means 'stars'.

Character — Portia

Portia takes control of her relationship with Bassanio. She called him her "lord", in Act 3, Scene 2, but now establishes her authority by threatening to cheat on him.

231 In Greek mythology, Argus was a giant with one hundred eyes. Even when Argus was sleeping, he kept most of his eyes open.

235-236 'And I'll sleep with his assistant, so take care when you leave me to my own devices.'

237-238 'Fine, go ahead. Don't let me catch him, though — if I do, I'll destroy his pen (i.e. penis).'

241 'enforcèd' means 'necessary'.

244-247 In other words — 'Did you hear that? When he looks into my eyes he sees a double reflection of himself. An oath sworn on a two-faced reflection isn't worth believing.'

Act Five

Act 5, Scene 1

251-252 'and if it weren't for the man who received your husband's ring, I would certainly have died'.

254 'advisedly' means 'knowingly'.

255 'surety' means 'guarantor'. Portia is saying that Antonio will be held responsible if Bassanio breaks his vow to her again.

Theme — Love

In the 16th century, a man was seen as weak if his wife cheated on him. Portia and Nerissa's claims would be very humiliating for their husbands if they were true.

264-265 'This is like fixing roads in the summer when they don't need it'.

266 A 'cuckold' is a man who has an unfaithful wife.

271-273 'Lorenzo can confirm that I left straight after you and that I've only just come back'.

Character — Portia

Portia doesn't just save Antonio's life — she also tells him his ships have returned to Venice safely. Her actions are mainly responsible for the play's happy ending.

280 'dumb' means 'speechless'.

289 'road' means 'harbour'.

Character — Antonio

Antonio's wealth is restored, but that doesn't end his sadness — he seems isolated at the end of the play, as he's the only main character left unmarried.

ANTONIO	I never more will break an oath with thee.
	(To Portia) I once did lend my body for his wealth; 250
	Which, but for him that had your husband's ring,
	Had quite miscarried: I dare be bound again,
	My soul upon the forfeit, that your lord
	Will never more break faith advisedly.
PORTIA	Then you shall be his surety. Give him this 255
	(Gives Antonio the ring) And bid him keep it
	better than the other.
ANTONIO	Here, lord Bassanio; swear to keep this ring.
BASSANIO	By heaven, it is the same I gave the doctor!
PORTIA	I had it of him: pardon me, Bassanio;
	For, by this ring, the doctor lay with me. 260
NERISSA	And pardon me, my gentle Gratiano;
	For that same scrubbèd boy, the doctor's clerk,
	In lieu of this last night did lie with me.
	(Shows him her ring)
GRATIANO	Why, this is like the mending of highways
	In summer, where the ways are fair enough: 265
	What, are we cuckolds ere we have deserved it?
PORTIA	Speak not so grossly. You are all amazed:
	Here is a letter; read it at your leisure; *(Hands*
	over a letter) It comes from Padua, from Bellario:
	There you shall find that Portia was the doctor, 270
	Nerissa there her clerk: Lorenzo here
	Shall witness I set forth as soon as you
	And even but now returned; I have not yet
	Entered my house. Antonio, you are welcome;
	And I have better news in store for you 275
	Than you expect: unseal this letter soon;
	(Gives him a letter)
	There you shall find three of your argosies
	Are richly come to harbour suddenly:
	You shall not know by what strange accident
	I chancèd on this letter.
ANTONIO	I am dumb. 280
BASSANIO	Were you the doctor and I knew you not?
GRATIANO	Were you the clerk that is to make me cuckold?
NERISSA	Ay, but the clerk that never means to do it,
	Unless he live until he be a man.
BASSANIO	Sweet doctor, you shall be my bed-fellow: 285
	When I am absent, then lie with my wife.
ANTONIO	Sweet lady, you have given me life and living;
	For here I read for certain that my ships
	Are safely come to road.
PORTIA	How now, Lorenzo!
	My clerk hath some good comforts too for you. 290
NERISSA	Ay, and I'll give them him without a fee.

Act 5, Scene 1

There do I give to you and Jessica,
From the rich Jew, a special deed of gift,
After his death, of all he dies possessed of.

LORENZO   Fair ladies, you drop manna in the way   295
Of starvèd people.

PORTIA   It is almost morning,
And yet I am sure you are not satisfied
Of these events at full. Let us go in;
And charge us there upon inter'gatories,
And we will answer all things faithfully.   300

GRATIANO   Let it be so: the first inter'gatory
That my Nerissa shall be sworn on is,
Whether till the next night she had rather stay,
Or go to bed now, being two hours to day:
But were the day come, I should wish it dark,   305
That I were couching with the doctor's clerk.
Well, while I live I'll fear no other thing
So sore as keeping safe Nerissa's ring.

Exeunt

Theme — Wealth

Lorenzo's claim that he and Jessica are "starvèd" suggests that they have already spent the stolen money recklessly.

295 In the Old Testament, 'manna' is the food that miraculously appears when Moses and the Israelites are on the brink of starvation in the desert.

299 'inter'gatories' means 'questions'.

301-304 'the first question Nerissa will have to answer is whether she would rather wait until tomorrow to sleep with me, or go to bed now'.

306 'couching' means 'sleeping'.

Shakespeare's Techniques

This is a pun on the word "ring", which refers to the female genitalia as well as the ring Nerissa gives Gratiano. This gives the play a humorous ending.

Shakespeare's Techniques — Form

The Merchant of Venice is a comedy, so it's important for Shakespeare to bring the play to a light-hearted conclusion after the drama and intensity of Act 4. All elements of a tragedy disappear in Act 5 — the play becomes much more like a typical Shakespearean comedy:

- The action is dominated by dramatic irony and comic misunderstandings. It's enjoyable for the audience to watch Bassanio and Gratiano try to talk their way out of trouble when the audience knows it's all a trick.

- Shylock isn't present in the final act. This stops the audience dwelling on his fate and allows love to become the main focus of the plot.

- The play finishes with a pun. This emphasises the joyful atmosphere of the ending.

Act Five

Act Five — Practice Questions

Quick Questions

1) Who was...
   a) Cressida   b) Diana   c) Argus?

2) What is Lancelet doing when he shouts "Sola, sola! Wo ha, ho! Sola, sola!"?

3) Who says "I am never merry when I hear sweet music"?

4) Why doesn't Portia want anyone to mention that she's been away?

5) How do Portia and Nerissa establish their authority over Bassanio and Gratiano?

6) What is meant by the word 'cuckold'?

7) What is the good news that Portia reveals to Antonio?

8) What does Lorenzo describe as "manna"? Why?

In-depth Questions

1) Explain how Shakespeare makes Lorenzo and Jessica seem close in this scene.

2) How does Shakespeare make Bassanio sound like a courtly lover in this scene?

3) Compare Bassanio and Gratiano's attitudes to their rings.
   What do their attitudes suggest about them as characters?

4) Why do you think Portia and Nerissa tell their husbands they've slept with other men?

5) Do you think Bassanio learns his lesson after being tricked by Portia? Explain your answer.

6) Why do you think Shakespeare leaves Shylock out of this scene?

7) Explain how Shakespeare creates dramatic irony in this scene.

8) Find an example of natural imagery from this scene and explain its effect.

9) Reread Act 5, Scene 1 (lines 70-88). Rewrite these lines in modern English.

10) Write some instructions for a set designer describing how you want Belmont to look
    in Act 5, Scene 1. Think about the sort of atmosphere you want the set to create.

Act Five

Practice Questions

Quick Questions

1) Why does Antonio borrow money from Shylock?

2) Find a moment in the play when the atmosphere is...
   a) tense   b) light-hearted   c) sorrowful.

3) Which two suitors fail the casket test?

4) "Never so rich a gem / Was set in worse than gold" is an example of what type of imagery?

5) Why can't Antonio repay Shylock in time?

6) Give three words that best describe Shylock's personality.

7) Why does Portia go to Venice?

8) Name three characters who wear disguises in the play.

Character Questions

1) Is Antonio's sadness resolved by the end of the play? Explain your answer.

2) Do you think Bassanio is a trustworthy character? Why / why not?

3) How does Shakespeare make Shylock seem like a bloodthirsty character?

4) Explain how Portia is presented as a strong-willed character.

5) Explain why the Prince of Morocco and the Prince of Aragon fail the casket test.

6) To what extent can Jessica be viewed as a selfish character? Explain your answer.

7) Explain how Shakespeare makes Lorenzo seem like a passionate character.

8) How does Shakespeare present the relationship between Gratiano and Nerissa?

9) Discuss the role of Lancelet in the play.

10) How does Shakespeare present the character of the Duke?

Practice Questions

Theme Questions

1) How does Shakespeare present seeking revenge as a bad idea?

2) Do you think the Christian characters are merciful to Shylock? Explain why / why not.

3) Do you think Bassanio has more than one reason for marrying Portia? Explain your answer.

4) Explain how romantic love comes into conflict with male friendship in the play.

5) Compare Portia and Jessica's relationships with their fathers.
   What do their relationships suggest about love between family members?

6) How is the casket test used to explore ideas about reality and appearance?

7) Do you think the idea that appearances can be deceiving applies to the characters
   as well as the caskets? Explain your answer.

8) How does Shakespeare present wealth in the play?

9) Is Shylock the only character to experience prejudice? Explain your answer.

10) Explain whether you think the play is driven more by love or hatred.

Technique Questions

1) How does Shakespeare use different settings in the play?

2) Identify a turning point in the mood of the play, then explain how the mood changes.

3) Discuss the role of dramatic irony in *The Merchant of Venice*.

4) Explain how Shakespeare uses structure to create tension in the play.

5) Find three mythological images from separate scenes and describe each of their effects.

6) Explain how Shakespeare uses language to create humour in the play.

7) Discuss the symbolism of rings in *The Merchant of Venice*.

8) Explain how Shakespeare uses music to create different atmospheres in the play.

9) Do you think *The Merchant of Venice* should be classed as a comedy? Explain your answer.

The Characters in 'The Merchant of Venice'

Phew! You should be an expert on *The Merchant of Venice* by now. But if you want a bit of light relief and a quick recap of what happens in the play, read through *The Merchant of Venice — The Cartoon...*

Antonio

Shylock

Bassanio

Portia

Nerissa

Gratiano

Jessica

Lorenzo

Salerio

Solanio

Lancelet

The Duke

Tubal

William Shakespeare's 'The Merchant of Venice'

EPMV41